Abortion
Understanding the Debate

Kathlyn Gay

Enslow Publishers, Inc.

40 Industrial Road   PO Box 38
Box 398   Aldershot
Berkeley Heights, NJ 07922   Hants GU12 6BP
USA   UK

http://www.enslow.com

Library of Congress Cataloging-in-Publication Data

Gay, Kathlyn.
    Abortion : understanding the debate / Kathlyn Gay.
      p. cm. — (Issues in focus)
    Summary: An overview of the issues surrounding the debate
over whether abortion should be permitted by law, and under what
circumstances.
    Includes bibliographical references and index.
    ISBN 0-7660-2162-9 (alk. paper)
    1. Abortion—United States—Juvenile literature. 2. Pro-life
movement—United States—Juvenile literature. 3. Pro-choice
movement—United States—Juvenile literature. [1. Abortion.]
I. Title. II. Issues in focus (Hillside, N.J.)
HQ767.5.U5G387 2004
363.4'6—dc22

                               2003015065

Printed in the United States of America

10 9 8 7 6 5 4 3 2

To Our Readers: We have done our best to make sure all Internet
Addresses in this book were active and appropriate when we went to
press. However, the author and the publisher have no control over and
assume no liability for the material available on those Internet sites or on
links to other Web sites. Any comments or suggestions can be sent by
e-mail to comments@enslow.com or to the address on the back cover.

Illustration Credits: All photos are from AP/Wide World.

Cover Illustration: AP/Wide World.

Contents

Author's Note

Some of the names and the stories in this book are fictional, but they are based on the words, feelings, and experiences of people who have been affected by the abortion question. When a fictional name is used, it is noted with an asterisk.

1

Struggling With Abortion Dilemmas

Like many teenagers, Andrea* was adamantly opposed to abortion. In her view, abortion was the same as murder. She felt the same way when she got pregnant at the age of fifteen. But after weeks of worry, she decided she was too young to have a child and could not complete her pregnancy. She believes she made the right choice, but is unhappy about her decision. "It makes me cry," she said.

Another fifteen-year-old made just the opposite decision. She was date raped and became pregnant. Although she was urged

*indicates a fictional name

5

to have an abortion, she could not go through with it. Instead, she chose to give her baby up for adoption.

If a birth mother, such as the young woman just described, decides to release her baby for adoption, she signs legal forms that end her rights to the child and gives her consent to the adoption. The father, if known and willing, also signs the consent forms. The procedures vary with each state, but when an adoption is final, the child legally becomes the son or daughter of the adoptive parents.

In another instance, Barbara,* who had had an abortion at age fifteen, became pregnant again two years later. But she decided against a second abortion, and continued her pregnancy, seeing a doctor for prenatal care. About three months into her pregnancy, she had an ultrasound and was thrilled to see the outline of the baby's limbs and even its nose. Barbara became a proud mother—not proud of having a child at age seventeen, but delighted that her child was alive and healthy. She pointed out that a teenager who has a baby may face tough times, and may not be able to graduate from high school. But it is possible to go on as Barbara did, managing her life and that of her child.

Each year most pregnant women in the United States never consider an abortion and give birth. Although twenty-one out of every thousand women of reproductive age had an abortion in 2000,[1] the number of abortions has declined steadily since the 1990s.

A steady drop in teen pregnancies helps reduce the total number of abortions each year. The U.S. Centers for Disease Control and Prevention (CDC) believes

Teen pregnancy often involves difficult choices. This young woman, who placed her baby for adoption, talks with other students about her decision.

wider and better use of contraceptives, or birth control—mechanical means to prevent pregnancy—is a major factor in reducing pregnancies. There are numerous birth control methods whose effectiveness depends on consistent and correct use. Among them are condoms, contraceptive creams or jellies inserted into the vagina, diaphragms or caps that cover the cervix (opening to the womb), oral contraceptives (known as "the pill"), and implants of a hormone that prevents the ovaries from releasing eggs.

One birth control method that is 100 percent effective is abstinence—not having vaginal intercourse. Abstinence education programs, funded by the federal government, have been implemented in communities nationwide. The U.S. Department of Health and Human Services reported in 2002 that these programs are changing teenage views about sex and helping to reduce teen pregnancies. The programs teach that abstinence from sexual activity as an unmarried person is "the only certain way to avoid out-of-wedlock pregnancy, sexually transmitted diseases and other associated health problems." The programs also teach that abstinence outside marriage is "the expected standard for all school age children."[2]

A sixteen-year-old who grew up in a poor neighborhood in Atlanta has chosen abstinence. She is well aware that many teenage girls have babies, and then their children become teenage mothers themselves. She told a *New York Times* reporter that she wants "to break that cycle. . . . I have a life, and I do plan on living it."[3]

Choices

A full-term pregnancy usually lasts from thirty-nine to forty weeks, but it can end accidentally if a woman's body rejects a fetus (a developing human in the womb) because of biological reasons, disease, or injury. When this happens, she has what is technically called a spontaneous abortion (commonly known as a miscarriage). A miscarriage can be a traumatic experience for many women, but because it is accidental, it is not usually the subject of debate. However, deliberately choosing to end a pregnancy—called an induced or elective abortion—is the focus of major health, social, moral, and legal issues.

An induced abortion, within specified limits, has been legal in the United States for more than thirty years. It is a procedure that usually takes place under the supervision of a physician in a doctor's office, health clinic, or hospital.

Women choose abortion for various reasons. They may be single and not want anyone to know about their pregnancy. They may feel that having a baby would disrupt school or work responsibilities. Women may be having problems with their intimate partners or within their marriages. Perhaps a couple already has children and does not want any more or cannot afford a child. Not everyone would agree, however, that these are valid reasons for choosing abortion.

Medical technology has also had an influence on abortion decisions. Many pregnant women have prenatal tests to determine whether there is a potential for abnormalities such as genetic diseases, mental retardation, or physical handicaps. An estimated 125,000 American women each year undergo amniocentesis, a procedure in which a doctor inserts a thin needle through a woman's abdomen to extract fluid from the amniotic sac that holds the fetus. The fluid is analyzed to examine chromosomes for disorders. If the results of amniocentesis show an abnormality, some women may choose to have an abortion. Yet others may choose to continue a pregnancy and learn how to care for a child with physical or mental disabilities. Or a woman might opt to have surgery or treatment of abnormalities while the fetus is in the womb.

Some Dilemmas

Some women may be sure they want an abortion and have no qualms about their choice, but others find the decision difficult to make or change their minds and do not go ahead with the procedure. Teenagers and

Many programs seek to reduce teen pregnancy by promoting abstinence— completely refraining from having sexual intercourse. Teens at an abstinence rally in Mississippi wear "Just Wait" pins.

women who write about their abortion decisions and post them on Internet sites frequently advise pregnant teenagers to carefully think about what they want to do. Some who have had abortions contend that teenagers should make their own decisions and not let others decide for them. Others describe their conflicting feelings and views about abortion and their concern that they would feel guilty if they ended their pregnancies. Still others express relief and gratitude that the choice to have an abortion was available for them so that they had a chance to get on with their lives.

Conversely, women also post numerous stories relating the many reasons they could not proceed with an abortion. Some who have ended their pregnancies describe remorse and feelings of deep shame for their actions.

An unplanned pregnancy causes numerous dilemmas for countless women, but problems vary with individuals and their circumstances. In some cases, decisions are determined by economic, social, health, family issues, or religious beliefs.

Money, or the lack of it, is a factor that may determine whether an abortion takes place. Some women are able to get financial support from their partners or families to carry a pregnancy to term, while others get little if any help. One young woman, Carol,* whose job at a fast-food restaurant barely paid for her living expenses, could not support a child. Although she feared her boyfriend would desert her if she had an abortion, just the opposite happened. The two later married.

Another young man also supported an abortion for his girlfriend. In his view his entire life would have changed if he had had to support a child.

On the other hand, a teenage couple, Dee* and Eric,* decided against abortion when Dee became pregnant. Instead, they married, managed to get jobs and attend night school. The couple's parents helped out by providing living quarters, some income, and baby-sitting services.

Dilemmas also occur because of psychological or physical problems. Perhaps a pregnant woman is severely depressed and suicidal, or she may have heart disease, diabetes, epilepsy, or other serious physical condition that could be aggravated—even to the point of being life-threatening—if a pregnancy is continued. In some instances, medical tests may show that a fetus has a serious physical disorder.

Rape and incest are other factors that can lead to abortion. People who support abortion rights contend that any woman who becomes pregnant as a result of rape or incest should be able to end the pregnancy. From the pro-choice point of view, not allowing an abortion would be equal to another assault—by a society that sentences a woman to carry the fetus of her abuser and live with a reminder of the terror she suffered. In an anonymous article, a journalist whose daughter was abducted, gang-raped, dumped from a car, and returned home in hysterics wrote that as soon as he and his wife realized that his daughter was pregnant, they *all* knew what to do. He wrote,

> The fetus didn't mean anything to me. I have no love for something that was brought about by

horror, terror, and attack. . . . My wife and I took my daughter for the abortion and brought her home. The abortion was not a traumatic experience. It was the end to a traumatic experience.[4]

However, antiabortionists claim that abortion constitutes a second assault on a woman who has become pregnant through rape or incest. In their view, aborting an unborn child is the same as an attack on an innocent person. They believe that a woman can find healing if she carries a pregnancy to term.

One young woman, Fern,* was a victim of incest. She was raped by her father numerous times. When she became pregnant, her father was enraged and

Fetal surgery is rare, but some babies have benefited from new procedures to treat abnormalities or disease before birth. This baby had surgery while still in the womb to correct spina bifida, a serious disorder.

demanded that she have an abortion. Because of her religious beliefs, Fern was convinced that abortion was murder. She thought that even in the painful circumstances, it was better to have a baby than to kill it. However, her father made her get an abortion.

Fern believes she should have done more to fight her father and save her child's life. The pain and guilt she felt over the incest were intensified by the abortion experience. She sees herself as having been hurt and violated by the doctor who performed the abortion as well as by the father who raped her.

Many Americans have strong religious beliefs about abortion, which may determine what they will do about an unplanned pregnancy. A recent study published in the *Journal of Youth and Adolescence* found that teen abortion rates are lower among those who have strong religious beliefs than among those who consider themselves nonreligious or do not often attend religious services. In the eighteen states studied, communities in which abortion rates were low also were found to have a high number of people who are religious believers.[5]

Nevertheless, some religious teenagers do opt for abortion. But they may be anxious—even terrified—when they have to face their families. This may be especially difficult for a teenager like Galen,* whose family accepts the current Catholic teaching that abortion is morally wrong. When Galen had an abortion, she felt she would be punished for the rest of her life.

Making a Decision

Clearly, a pregnant woman can be persuaded, forced, or intimidated to have or not have an abortion. Or she can make her decision without a lot of outside pressure, though such a decision is not made in a vacuum. A woman may be influenced by what she knows or understands about abortion in American society.

There have long been pro and con opinions about abortion, and abortion issues have been argued for decades in the United States among politicians and lawmakers, in the courts, at rallies, within families, and between people. Groups and individuals have frequently taken a public stand on one side or the other. Since the 1970s, many people who oppose abortion have called themselves "pro-life," while many who support a woman's right to choose an abortion have called themselves "pro-choice."

People in both the pro-life and pro-choice groups come from varied backgrounds. For example, pro-life advocates may have no religious faith; they may be feminists (those who advocate for women's rights), scientists, lawyers, doctors, nurses, teachers, or people in any number of other professions and jobs. Pro-choice supporters may have strong religious beliefs; they may be members of diverse professions or work at varied jobs. Some, but certainly not all, pro-life and pro-choice views will be covered in detail in later chapters. But first it is important to know the history of the procedure as well as what is involved in an abortion—how it is performed, who the providers are, and where abortions take place.

History of Abortion and Abortion Laws

For centuries, women who faced unwanted pregnancies have resorted to abortion, regardless of religious bans or laws against the practice. Ancient Chinese, Egyptians, Greeks, and Romans, for example, used poisonous herbs to induce abortion, as did tribal groups worldwide. Seldom was such a practice condemned.

In some societies, abortion was often a form of birth control—a way to maintain a stable population. In addition, in ancient times, some couples used wads of cloth soaked in acidic brews that killed sperm and condoms "made from animal membranes or oiled silk" to prevent conception.[1]

Although early Christians opposed abortion after "animation," or the time when the fetus first moves in the womb—later called "quickening"—they did not condemn abortion before quickening. In their view, the fetus came alive and became a living soul "forty days after conception for a boy and eighty days after conception for a girl." Catholic theologian St. Augustine (A.D.354–430) declared, "There cannot yet be said to be a live soul in a body that lacks sensation," thus it was believed that an early abortion was not homicide.[2] This view prevailed until 1869, when Roman Catholic Pope Pius IX decreed that there was no difference between an animated and nonanimated fetus and banned abortion at any time.

Abortion in Early America

In early America, common (unwritten) law regarding abortion was patterned after English law. Generally, a pregnant woman could choose to have an abortion before quickening. Women who ended their pregnancies usually did so because they were not married or had been involved in an affair outside marriage and wanted to avoid disgrace.

Colonial women who wanted to end a pregnancy were likely to use herbal brews made from plants found in the woods or grown in their gardens. If a woman's menstrual period was late and she suspected she was pregnant (she had no medical way to confirm this), she might brew a combination of two or three herbs to drink several times a day. The brew reportedly acted as an abortifacient—a drug to end a pregnancy. It was said to bring on uterine contractions, which expelled a fetus and restored menstrual bleeding. Some plants also had contraceptive qualities; they contained chemicals that hindered the sperm from reaching the egg or stopped a fertilized egg from implanting in the uterus.

Today, books warn about herbal teas and mixtures that are said to be abortifacients. As *The Abortion Resource Handbook* notes:

> Historical and anecdotal evidence suggests that certain herbs and plants can, in fact, induce abortions. *However, the procedures and methods used are neither safe nor reliable.* **Some herbs are highly toxic and, when taken improperly, can cause heavy cramping and bleeding, nausea, diarrhea, high blood pressure, heart failure, and death** (emphasis in original).[3]

An expert on botanical medicine reinforces this warning: Women who take herbs to induce abortion are actually "creating such high toxicity that their own body is unable to sustain the pregnancy." An herb that works as an abortifacient is doing so "because it's poisoning the mother."[4]

Abortion in the 1800s

Abortion before quickening continued to be an accepted practice in the United States into the nineteenth century. Historian Timothy Crumrin points out that Midwestern women of the 1800s consulted medical books such as *Buchan's Domestic Medicine,* which advised laxatives and a mixture of herbs to induce abortion.[5]

Some women certainly tried these and other home

remedies and were able to end their pregnancies. But they had no guarantee that any one method or a combination of methods would work. Recipes for herbal abortion were not scientifically tested, and even today have not been rigorously examined.

By the 1830s and 1840s, abortifacients—herbal products and over-the-counter drugs—were widely used, and some states passed laws to ban them. These laws were actually designed to protect women from poisoning themselves. However, the drugs were still marketed in drugstores and sold by doctors, mail-order companies, midwives (who assisted in childbearing), and "natural healers" (those practicing nontraditional health care). If medications failed, wealthy and middle-class women could go to their doctors for abortions before quickening. Poor women seldom could afford this option.

By the middle of the nineteenth century, an increasing number of middle-class married women—primarily Protestants of white northern European ancestry—had been ending pregnancies to limit the size of their families. With birth rates declining among this group, some Protestant leaders feared they would be outnumbered by immigrant groups of other religions (particularly Roman Catholics) and by people of color. As author Leslie J. Reagan explains,

> The visible use of abortion by middle-class married
> women . . . generated anxieties among American
> men of the same class. . . . Antiabortion activists
> pointed out that immigrant families, many of them
> Catholic, were larger and would soon outpopulate
> native-born [whites] and threaten their political

power. . . . White male patriotism demanded that maternity be enforced among white Protestant women.[6]

Some native-born white people labeled abortion "race suicide," and began to call for abortion bans. Other groups advocated bans because they were concerned about the women's movement, which at that time was campaigning for women's suffrage and other rights. These groups "worried that continuing access to abortion would permit women to stray from their traditional roles as wives and mothers."[7]

Physicians also became vocal about stopping abortions, and the American Medical Association (AMA), which had formed in 1847, began to say that abortion should be made a crime. In 1857, Dr. Horatio Storer, an obstetrician and gynecologist, led the AMA on an antiabortion campaign. One AMA report said that a woman who had an abortion was selfish and immoral, and "unmindful of the course marked out for her by Providence."[8]

However, Storer and the AMA primarily supported abortion bans for medical reasons. In the first place, antiseptics and other medications were not widely available, and women died of infections or excessive bleeding from their abortions. Physicians were concerned about increasing abortion-related injuries and deaths due to botched procedures, whether performed by an unlicensed abortionist or by a pregnant woman herself. Doctors also wanted to gain control of childbearing, taking over the traditional practices of midwives and other nonmedical persons who cared for pregnant women. After Storer initiated "the physicians' crusade against abortion," he wrote two antiabortion books that contributed to the success of the crusade and passage of laws banning abortion.[9]

A federal statute, the Comstock Act, passed in 1873, also had an effect on restricting abortions. The act was named for Anthony Comstock, a salesman and religious zealot who set himself up as the moral guardian of Americans' reading material. He became secretary and special agent of the New York Society for Suppression of Vice and was appointed post office inspector of New York. In that position, Comstock was instrumental in making it a criminal offense to send what he called "obscene," "lewd," "indecent," or "immoral" publications through the U.S. mails. He labeled birth control and abortion information obscene.

The act remained a federal law, and it is still on the books with some modifications. In 1971, the birth control ban was deleted, but the ban on distributing abortion information remained, although it has not been enforced. U.S. Representative Henry Hyde of Illinois attempted to retain portions of the Comstock Act by inserting the Communications Decency Act into the new Telecommunications Act of 1996. However, in 1997 the U.S. Supreme Court ruled in *Reno* v. *ACLU* that the federal Communications Decency Act is an unconstitutional restriction on free speech, affirming a lower court decision.

The Comstock Act and other antiabortion efforts during the 1800s created enough leverage that by the end of the nineteenth century, abortion was illegal in all states—though most states allowed abortion to save the pregnant woman's life.

The Birth Control Issue

Although abortion was a major political issue during the late 1800s and early 1900s, most feminists (advocates for women's rights) of the time focused on gaining women's right to vote, overcoming female oppression, and accessing information on birth control. Society expected females to bear and nurture children and to care for their husbands and the home. Thus it was common for many women to give birth each year, wearing out their own bodies and producing sick infants.

Feminists strongly supported birth control and opposed abortion, arguing that it was not only dangerous but also an indication of female oppression. They believed that if women could control their pregnancies, abortion would not be necessary. "The birth controllers contrasted the danger of abortion to the safety of contraceptives and argued strenuously against abortion," wrote Leslie J. Reagan.[10]

The main concern of feminists was providing access to birth control services for all women. In spite of laws against birth control, wealthy women were able to get contraceptives from their doctors, and with enough money could find providers who would perform illegal abortions. But poor women could not afford private doctors and did not have access to reproductive health services. Feminist and anarchist Emma Goldman, who provided midwife services for poor women, noted that many resorted to "fantastic methods" to end a pregnancy, "jumping off tables, rolling on the floor, massaging the stomach, drinking nauseating concoctions, and using blunt instruments."[11] Along with Goldman, activists such as Margaret Sanger and Mary Ware Dennett worked to set up birth control clinics to serve women whom they termed "the less fortunate."

Yet many women had little say over the use of contraceptives, particularly if their husbands or partners demanded sexual relations without using any birth control measures. It was not unusual for women with numerous children to seek and find ways to have abortions in order to prevent births and protect their own health. Women who had had difficult pregnancies and problems in childbirth feared that they risked death if they delivered more children. Frequently these women went to birth control clinics hoping to end their pregnancies, but clinic personnel informed them that "birth control did not mean abortion." Nevertheless, many women of the time "did not make a distinction between contraception and abortion, but saw them as part of the same project—a way to avoid unwanted childbearing,"[12] according to Leslie Reagan.

Illegal Abortions

By 1900 most abortions were outlawed except to save a pregnant woman's life, but that did not prevent some women from obtaining an abortion. As David J.

Margaret Sanger was one of the founders of the birth control movement, which sought to give women control over child-bearing. She was arrested for running a birth control clinic.

Garrow, Emory University School of Law professor, pointed out:

> A medical abortion was reasonably easy to obtain for women who had money and connections, and extremely difficult for women who did not have money and connections—[this] is a consistent thread . . . from the early 1900s right up to the present time.[13]

Some women were so determined to end a pregnancy that they used whatever means available, even if it meant risking death. It was not unusual for women to poke sharp instruments into themselves trying to open up the uterus and end a pregnancy. According to the American Civil Liberties Union (ACLU):

> In the early part of [the twentieth century], an estimated 800,000 illegal abortions took place annually [in the United States], resulting in 8,000–17,000 women's deaths each year. Thousands of other women suffered severe consequences short of death, including perforations of the uterus, cervical wounds, serious bleeding, infections, poisoning, shock, and gangrene.[14]

In Canada, laws were even more restrictive than in the United States. "From 1869 to 1969 in Canada, abortion for any reason was a crime punishable by life imprisonment," according to *No Choice: Canadian Women Tell Their Stories of Illegal Abortion.*[15] As a result of these restrictions, one woman living in rural Canada found her own way to end a pregnancy. She already had two children and "was afraid to have another child in an isolated place, one hundred miles from a doctor." Years later her daughter described her mother's desperate actions: "She went out to the fields and guided the plough, pulled by two oxen, until she had so strained herself that she miscarried."[16]

While this woman did not suffer serious health problems and later gave birth to a daughter, others were not as fortunate. A nurse who tended rural women after they attempted to abort their pregnancies noted in an interview that the women

> would jump off the roof of the house, or they would fall off a horse. But most of all they would do themselves harm by using instruments of some sort, to make the blood come. They thought by bleeding they would get rid of it.[17]

As Emma Goldman observed, women in the United States used similar methods to abort during the 1800s and most of the 1900s. A metal clothes hanger was often an instrument used for a self-induced abortion, a dangerous practice that could kill or seriously injure a woman.

When the now-famous entertainer Whoopi Goldberg realized in 1968 at the age of fourteen that she was pregnant, she "panicked." In an interview for the book *The Choices We Made,* she said:

> I sat in hot baths. I drank these strange concoctions girls told me about. . . . I got violently ill. . . . At that moment I was more afraid of having to explain to anybody what was wrong than of going to the park with a hanger. . . . Afterwards, I was in a lot of pain. I think the hanger worked, 'cause I then had a period several days later.[18]

Changing Abortion Laws

Unlike the early feminists, women's rights organizations of the 1960s began efforts to change restrictive state abortion laws. Reforms did not occur easily or readily, and when most states lifted bans, abortion was only allowed to save the life of a woman or in cases of rape and incest. However, during the decade, twelve states—Arkansas, California, Colorado, Delaware, Georgia, Kansas, Maryland, New Mexico, North Carolina, Oregon, South Carolina, and Virginia—changed their laws, basing them on a model established by the American Law Institute. The model law permitted abortions to be performed by licensed physicians to protect the woman's physical and mental health, in cases of fetal defects, or when the pregnancy resulted from rape or incest.[19] In 1970, New York, Hawaii, Alaska, and Washington also repealed their abortion laws, so that the procedure became more widely available, although some restrictions remained.

After abortion was legalized nationally in 1973, the mortality rate for women who ended their pregnancies steadily dropped. As the ACLU explained:

> Abortion services moved from the back alleys into hygienic facilities staffed by health professionals. High-quality training, the ability of professionals openly to share their expertise with one another, and the development of specialized clinics all enhanced the safety of abortion services.[20]

Today, deaths related to legal abortions occur very rarely—approximately one death per one hundred thousand legal induced abortions.[21] The Alan Guttmacher Institute used statistics from its own research and the CDC for a report that pointed out that childbirth poses a greater risk of death—about eleven times greater—than abortion. A CDC report stated that each year, 300–500 pregnancy-related deaths are reported in the United States, although "another 500–800 such are probably not identified as pregnancy related."[22] Death risks from abortion increase as pregnancy continues, "from 1 death for every 500,000 abortions at 8 or fewer weeks to 1 per 27,000 at 16–20 weeks and 1 per 8,000 at 21 or more weeks," according to the Alan Guttmacher Institute.[23]

The *Roe* v. *Wade* Decision

The highly controversial *Roe* v. *Wade* case, which legalized abortion nationally in 1973, was named for a pregnant single woman, Norma McCorvey of Texas, who used the fictitious name Jane Roe, and Texas Attorney General Henry Wade. Wade defended a Texas law that made abortions illegal except to save the life of the pregnant woman.

In the early 1970s, McCorvey worked only occasionally at low-paying jobs and did not want to have a child. But McCorvey had no choice; she continued her pregnancy and agreed to give up her child for adoption. While making adoption arrangements, she learned that civil rights lawyers were planning to challenge the Texas abortion law and needed someone to file a lawsuit. McCorvey agreed to be that person. To protect her privacy, her lawyers used the name Jane Roe in the lawsuit.

In 1973, the Supreme Court in *Roe* v. *Wade* struck down state laws that severely restricted abortion, declaring them unconstitutional because they did not protect a woman's right of privacy. Although the right of privacy is not explicitly mentioned in the Constitution, "a right of personal privacy, or a guarantee of certain areas or zones of privacy, does exist under the Constitution," the Court ruled.

The Court based its decision in part on an earlier ruling, *Griswold* v. *Connecticut* (1965), which struck down a state law that prohibited giving married couples information on birth control. In that case, the Court ruled that marital privacy was a fundamental right guaranteed by the Constitution and government could not interfere with that privacy.

Many legal scholars say this decision prompted lawyers to extend that argument to cover a woman's fundamental right to choose whether or not to continue an unwanted pregnancy. The roots of that right can be found in the First, Fourth, Fifth, Ninth, and Fourteenth Amendments to the Constitution. In the opinion of the Court, the right of privacy is "broad enough to encompass a woman's decision whether or not to terminate her pregnancy."[24]

In the 1973 *Roe* v. *Wade* decision, the Supreme Court held that:

- During the first trimester (three months) of pregnancy, a woman had the right to an abortion for any reason.

- During the second trimester of pregnancy, states may pass laws regulating abortion to protect a woman's health.

- During the third trimester of pregnancy, when the fetus can live outside the womb, states may pass laws to protect the fetus by prohibiting abortion except to preserve the health or life of the pregnant woman.

In another case, *Doe* v. *Bolton*, the Court ruled that a judgment regarding a woman's health should include more than physical well-being. The Court determined that health also involved emotional and psychological conditions, family situation, and age as "relevant to the well-being of the patient."[25]

Restrictions

In 1995, more than two decades after her involvement in *Roe* v. *Wade*, Norma McCorvey in 1995 renounced her participation and said she had converted to Catholicism. She began an antiabortion ministry called Roe No More. In addition, since the *Roe* decision, opposition groups have formed to campaign for restrictions or complete bans on abortion.

Some restrictive laws and regulations have been passed. For example, the Hyde Amendment (named for U.S. Representative Henry Hyde) passed in 1977 to prevent federal Medicaid funds from being used for abortions. Under the Medicaid program, federal and state governments share the cost of medical care for many of the poorest Americans.

Norma McCorvey used the name "Jane Roe" in the landmark Roe v. Wade case, in which the Supreme Court struck down laws against abortion. However, McCorvey later converted to Catholicism and has since worked as an antiabortion activist.

Selected U.S. Supreme Court Decisions After *Roe* v. *Wade*

- 1973—*Doe* v. *Bolton*. The Supreme Court found a Georgia law unconstitutional that required a doctor's judgment regarding abortion to be confirmed by a committee or by another doctor; the Court also ruled it unconstitutional to require abortions to be performed in a hospital.

- 1977—*Maher* v. *Roe*. The Supreme Court upheld the right of a state to refuse to use public medical funds for abortion.

- 1989—*Webster* v. *Reproductive Health Services*. The Court upheld a Missouri law that public employees and public facilities could not be used to perform or assist in abortions unnecessary to save the mother's life; prohibited counseling to have an abortion; and required physicians to perform viability tests upon women in their twentieth (or more) week of pregnancy.

- 1990—*Hodgson* v. *Minnesota*; *Ohio* v. *Akron Center*. In both cases, the Court ruled that states can require parental notification if a minor requests an abortion and can require a 48-hour waiting period after notification prior to the abortion.

Selected U.S. Supreme Court Decisions After *Roe* v. *Wade* (continued)

- 1992—*Planned Parenthood of Eastern Pennsylvania v. Casey*. The Court upheld most of a Pennsylvania law that requires that a woman give her informed consent prior to an abortion procedure and that she be given certain information at least 24 hours before the procedure.

- 1994 (upheld 1997)—*Madsen et al. v. Women's Health Center*. The Court ruled that antiabortionists cannot cross a fixed buffer zone around abortion clinics to stage protests.

- 2000—*Stenberg v. Carhart*. The Supreme Court upheld a district court's ruling that a Nebraska "partial-birth abortion" law was unconstitutional because it did not provide protection for the health of a woman.

- 2001—*Ferguson v. City of Charleston, South Carolina*. The Court ruled that a hospital that tested pregnant women for drug use without their knowledge violated the Fourth Amendment to the U.S. Constitution, which protects citizens against unreasonable searches.

In the 1980s, President Ronald Reagan tried to repeal Title X, a federal program that provides services such as contraceptive supplies, pelvic and breast examinations, blood pressure checks, pregnancy tests, and tests for sexually transmitted diseases (STDs) and HIV. Title X funds cannot be used for abortion services or referrals, but the program requires that a pregnant woman be offered "non-directive counseling," which includes providing information about "prenatal care and delivery; infant care, foster care or adoption; and pregnancy termination [ending a pregnancy]."[26] These medical services are available to Americans who want and need them but are unable to afford them without government assistance. Reagan hoped to send federal family planning funds to the states. Congress rejected the president's proposal and retained Title X as a federal program. To date, Title X still exists, but some members of Congress and President George W. Bush have attempted to reduce funding for the program or to eliminate it altogether.

Another Reagan administration order, dubbed the "global gag rule," was instituted in 1984 to ban taxpayer funding of abortion counseling in family planning organizations overseas. President Bill Clinton reversed the order eight years later. But President George W. Bush issued an executive order to reinstate the global gag rule on his third day in office. No family planning funds can be used overseas to advise women about the option of a legal abortion or to promote abortion as a method of family planning. In addition, U.S. funds cannot be used by organizations that participate in advocacy programs for legal abortions in their own countries or provide legal abortion services.

At the state level, numerous legislatures have passed laws that restrict abortion. But some of these laws have been challenged in court, and the Supreme Court has found some state laws unconstitutional.

3

Abortion Today

Most abortions in the United States occur before viability, or before a fetus is able to survive on its own—between twenty-one and twenty-eight weeks from conception. Conception is another term for fertilization, when the male spermatozoa (sperm) contacts a female ovum (egg) in a woman's fallopian tube and produces a single-celled organism known as a *zygote*. The fertilized egg must then find a place to continue developing. If the zygote attaches itself to the wall of a woman's uterus, it can grow to become an *embryo*, the stage of development about two weeks from

36

Abortion Statistics

Numerous statistics on abortion are released from various sources, but valid data on abortions nation-wide come from only two sources: the federal Centers for Disease Control and Prevention (CDC) and the privately funded Alan Guttmacher Institute (AGI).

The CDC has been collecting data since 1969 and depends on reports primarily from state health departments and from the District of Columbia and New York City. The AGI has been gathering informa-tion directly from abortion providers since 1974. Because of the differences in data collection methods, CDC and AGI statistics vary.

For example, CDC reported its data for 1998 (the most recent year for analysis of statistics) in 2002. The report showed that seventeen of every 1,000 American women between the ages of 15 and 44 had an abortion.[1] According to 2002 AGI statistics, "each year 2 out of every 100 women aged 15–44 have an abortion."[2]

conception to the eighth week, and then technically it will become a *fetus*.

Timing

The safest time for an abortion is during the first trimester—weeks one through twelve of a pregnancy. "The forty weeks of a pregnancy are generally viewed as three approximately three-month long trimesters," wrote Bernadine Healy, M.D., in her book on women's health.[3] Put another way, each trimester is about thirteen weeks long.[4]

During the second trimester (thirteen to twenty-six weeks into the pregnancy) and the third trimester (from twenty-seven weeks to birth), abortions are more complex and can pose health risks for women. In addition, third trimester, or late-term, abortions are much more restricted legally than those performed in the first two trimesters and are usually allowed only to protect the life or health of a pregnant woman. The health risks from continuing some pregnancies include hypertension (high blood pressure) that can cause a stroke, diabetes brought on by the pregnancy, and the possibility of infertility—inability to conceive. Abnormalities that are life-threatening to the fetus can also create health risks to a woman, especially if the fetus dies while in the uterus.

Teenagers "are more likely than older women to delay having an abortion until after 15 weeks of pregnancy, when medical risks associated with abortion increase significantly," according to the Alan Guttmacher Institute.[5] Why do teens wait so long to make a decision about abortion? Often they are in serious conflict about what to do. If they are single, some are afraid to tell parents, boyfriends, or others about their pregnancy. Some teenagers have reported that their parents have been furious with them, refusing to speak to them and treating them like outcasts.

Abortion or Birth Control?

Many couples use contraceptives—various methods of birth control—to prevent fertilization, or conception. But if birth control methods fail or are not used, some women opt for emergency contraception pills (ECPs). ECPs, sometimes called "morning-after pills," are like regular birth control pills that combine the hormones estrogen and progestin. Or the ECPs may contain only progestin. The U.S. Food and Drug Administration (FDA) approved their use for emergency contraception in 1997, and in 1998 and 1999, the agency approved products specifically designed as ECPs.

The first dose of ECPs must be taken within seventy-two hours of unprotected intercourse, and the second dose twelve hours later. The sooner the medication is taken after sex, the more effective it is.

A heavy dose of ECPs temporarily disrupts hormone patterns and delays or prevents an egg from being fertilized. The medication may also disturb the uterine lining so that a fertilized egg cannot be implanted. ECPs are considered safe and can effectively reduce the risk of pregnancy by 75 percent.

For years, doctors in hospital emergency rooms have prescribed ECPs for rape victims, but until recently, few physicians discussed this form of birth control with their regular patients. One of the reasons for the silence on the subject is the uncertainty about why the pills work as they do. Using emergency contraception is also more expensive than taking birth control pills on a regular basis because more ECPs are taken at one time. In addition, debates over whether

The birth control pill, introduced in the 1960s, is one method of contraception. Emergency contraception pills, similar to the regular pill, can be used after intercourse.

ECPs are an abortion method or means of birth control stifle open discussion on the subject. The use of ECPs has become controversial because it has been labeled an abortion procedure by those who oppose any artificial means to prevent a pregnancy and also by those who oppose the medication because it prevents implantation of a fertilized egg.

But due to advertising campaigns by women's health advocates, an increasing number of women, particularly young women and teenagers, are hearing about ECPs. Many doctors now say they would like ECPs to be available as over-the-counter medications, a position supported by the American Medical Association and the American College of Obstetricians and Gynecologists. Making it easier to obtain ECPs could reduce the total number of abortions each year, advocates say. If ECPs or other forms of birth control do not prevent a pregnancy, a medical or surgical abortion could be an option for some women. (A medical abortion is one caused by the use of medications rather than surgery.)

Medical Abortions

Medical abortions involve the use of abortifacients. Women can obtain various prescription medications for this purpose, take them home, and follow up with visits to their health-care provider. Many women choose medical abortion because it is more private and natural (more like a miscarriage) and also less invasive than surgery. However, if a medical abortion fails, surgery is necessary to end the pregnancy. "Candidates for medical abortion must be able to complete the regimen of drugs and to make between one and three visits to the medical provider," a Planned Parenthood question-and-answer sheet notes.[6]

One of the drugs, methotrexate, has been used since the 1950s for certain types of cancer treatment, and in recent years low doses have been prescribed for psoriasis (a skin disease), rheumatoid arthritis, and ectopic (or tubal) pregnancy. An ectopic pregnancy is a condition in which the egg and sperm join outside the uterus, often in a fallopian tube. A fetus cannot survive in a fallopian tube, and the condition is life-threatening for the pregnant woman. Such a condition can be detected early and the pregnancy ended with surgery or the use of methotrexate.

Research has shown that the drug also can stop the process by which the embryo attaches to the uterine wall, and since the early 1990s, methotrexate has been used with another drug, misoprostol, to end pregnancies. How does this work? There is no standard procedure, but usually a woman receives an injection (shot) of methotrexate or takes it in pill form during the first six weeks of a pregnancy. About a week after receiving methotrexate, she takes misoprostol, which induces contractions of the uterus that help expel the embryo. According to a study published in the *New England Journal of Medicine,* the combination of the two medications "represents a safe and effective alternative to invasive methods for the termination of early pregnancy."[7]

Another drug, mifepristone, formerly called RU-486, is also used in combination with misoprostol to end a pregnancy. Mifepristone (which has the brand name Mifeprex) blocks the action of a hormone needed to sustain a pregnancy. U.S. regulations limit the use of mifepristone to the first seven weeks after conception, although "in some parts of Europe and Asia hundreds of thousands of women are using it effectively and without incidence up to nine weeks of their pregnancies," reported author Ellen Chesler, director of the Open Society Institute's Program on Reproductive Health and Rights.[8]

Numerous medical reports show that mifepristone is safe and about 95 percent effective in ending a pregnancy. It was first developed in France in 1980, and has been tested and safely used by thousands of European women. The FDA banned import of the drug in 1989. Some claim that that ban was politically motivated because the drug is an abortifacient. Antiabortion groups have consistently opposed its manufacture in the United States, some calling it the "French death pill."[9] But despite political pressure, the FDA approved the drug in 2000.

However, mifepristone is still not widely used in the United States. This is partly because the FDA has said that only doctors who are trained to determine the duration of a pregnancy may prescribe it. They must also provide or make arrangements for a surgical abortion if mifepristone fails, because there is a possibility of birth defects if the pregnancy is not ended. Physicians must counsel patients about the abortion method and its cost. Preliminary reports suggest that most doctors charge more for medical than for surgical abortion.[10] In addition, some physicians are reluctant to prescribe mifepristone because it can cause painful cramping, nausea, and bleeding that may last several days. In one out of one hundred women, bleeding is so heavy that surgery is required to stop it, and doctors need to be available for such emergencies. Physicians must also report any serious adverse effects associated with the drug.[11]

Widespread use of mifepristone is also hindered because women sometimes confuse it with the ECP. A study by researchers at the University of Rochester, New York, found that women were concerned about whether mifepristone would work and whether it would be painful to use; they also wanted to know how it would affect their health and how they would feel afterward.[12]

Supporters of the drug maintain that its use will increase as more women learn about it. They also contend that mifepristone use will reduce the number of surgical abortions.

Surgical Procedures

A surgical abortion is usually performed in a doctor's office, health clinic, or hospital. More than 90 percent of all U.S. abortions are performed in nonhospital facilities. "In 2000, the cost of a nonhospital abortion with local anesthesia at 10 weeks of gestation [development] ranged from $150 to $4,000, and the average amount paid was $372," according to the Alan Guttmacher Institute.[13]

One process is called manual vacuum aspiration (MVA). In the procedure, a handheld suction syringe gently removes the embryo from the uterus. A local anesthetic, or painkiller, may be given, but might not always be necessary. An MVA takes place up to ten weeks from a woman's last menstrual period.

Suction curettage is another method, performed from about six to fourteen weeks; it usually requires anesthesia. The cervix, the opening of the uterus, is gradually dilated, or enlarged. As Planned Parenthood describes the procedure:

> After the opening is stretched, a tube, attached to a suction machine, is inserted through it into the uterus. The suction machine is turned on and the uterus is gently emptied. To be sure that

the uterus has been completely emptied after the suction tube has been removed, a curette (narrow metal loop) may be used to gently scrape the walls of the uterus.[14]

Though not common today, dilation and curettage (D&C) is another type of abortion procedure in which the cervix is dilated, or enlarged, and a curette is used to scrape the lining of the uterus. The procedure is also used when a woman has an incomplete miscarriage and tissue from the pregnancy that remains in the womb must be removed to prevent infection.

Late-Term Abortions

During the second trimester, the most common type of abortion is dilation and evacuation (D&E). In this procedure, an ultrasound first determines the size of the uterus and the length of the pregnancy. The cervix is dilated and the fetus and placenta are extracted, using forceps or other instruments. This procedure takes about thirty minutes.

Some abortions performed late in the second trimester and in the third trimester are variations of D&E. One method that has prompted emotional debates is intact dilation and extraction (D&X). Some have referred to it as "partial-birth abortion," a nonmedical term created to gain support for legal bans against the procedure.

Although D&X procedures can vary, the fetus is usually taken out feetfirst through the vagina, and suction is used to remove the brain and spinal fluid from the skull before extracting the entire dead fetus.[15] Such late-term abortions are not common, but they can be considered medically necessary if the fetus is dead or poses a severe threat to the life or health of a pregnant woman.

In some cases, an abortion late in pregnancy would be advised because a fetus is severely malformed or abnormal and cannot live outside the womb. One example is a case in which a fetus is diagnosed as anencephalic—lacking a forebrain or cranium, a fatal abnormality.

Hydrocephalus (water or fluid on the brain) is another abnormal condition that could prompt a late-term abortion. Sometimes a doctor can perform a surgical procedure to treat mild to moderate hydro-cephalus in the womb and save the fetus; very mild cases can also be treated after birth.

A fetus with advanced or severe hydrocephalus cannot be treated, however. In such a case, a fetus could have almost two gallons of fluid on the brain. Trying to give birth vaginally to a fetus with severe hydrocephalus could kill a woman, so a doctor would have to drain the fetal brain fluid and break down the skull in order to pull out the fetus without tearing the uterine passage. Another possibility might be a cesarean section (C-section), a major operation that involves cutting a woman's abdomen to deliver a baby. The C-section allows the newborn with severe hydro-cephalus to die on its own.

Aftereffects of Abortion

There have been numerous claims and counterclaims over the past few decades about the aftereffects of

Dr. Leroy Carhart challenged Nebraska's ban on D&X abortions. In 2000, the Supreme Court struck down the law. However, in 2003 abortion opponents in Congress voted to ban the procedure, which they call "partial-birth abortion."

abortion. The pro-life side contends that studies show that women suffer physical and psychological harm after an abortion. The pro-choice side argues that women who have had an abortion rarely have negative health effects—mental or physical.

Alleged health problems among women who have had abortions include (but are not limited to) infertility (problems in conceiving), later pregnancies that result in premature births, increased risk of breast cancer, depression, and post-abortion stress syndrome (PASS). PASS has been defined as a combination of reactions to abortion such as grief, nightmares about the abortion experience, sleep disorders, and other negative experiences that may last a few months or even years.

Although a great deal of research has been cited to prove or disprove one claim or another, a team of doctors at the University of North Carolina at Chapel Hill schools of medicine and public health declared that to date there are "no definitive studies" about the aftermath of abortion. In 2003, the university team reported in *Obstetrical and Gynecological Survey,* a professional journal, that the studies that have been conducted were small, the methods used were flawed, and conclusions were "often intertwined with the political agendas of their authors and publishers."

The scientists also concluded that women might not tell the whole truth about their reproductive histories, because ending a pregnancy often is an emotionally troubling choice. Politics of the issue also cloud results, with pro-life groups sometimes exaggerating claims about the negative effects of abortion and pro-choice groups minimizing them.

Finally, the researchers noted that "elective abortion must be studied . . . with vigor, given the frequency with which women choose to terminate a pregnancy." In their view, "before women undergo induced abortions, doctors should—as part of the informed consent process—offer them information" about the possible risk of preterm delivery and depression, and the slight possibility—*not yet proven*—of developing breast cancer later in life.[16]

4

The Abortion
Debate

Abortion is one of the most divisive issues in the United States, and over the years, numerous polls have been taken to determine American opinions on the subject. Some polls have shown that Americans are almost evenly divided in their opposition or support, although a majority of respondents have favored abortion when a mother's or fetus's health is in danger and in cases of rape or incest.

A 2003 ABC News–*Washington Post* poll showed that 57 percent of those surveyed favored abortion rights in all or most cases, while 69 percent opposed abortion by D&X

procedures.[1] Health on the Net Foundation stated in 2003:

> A poll of 1,218 adults conducted by the Pew Research Center [found] more than six in 10 Americans . . . opposed any effort by the U.S. Supreme Court to overturn its 30-year-old decision that permits legal abortions. . . . In a Gallup poll of 1,002 adults, 57 percent favored abortion under specific conditions, and one-quarter said abortion should be legal regardless of the circumstances.[2]

Whatever the polls say, there appears to be little middle ground between the pro and con forces. This is evident in the way groups try to advance their causes. For example, the term "pro-life," used by many antiabortionists to identify themselves, gives the impression that people who do not agree with them are against life and the living. On the other side, many who support abortion call themselves "pro-choice," which implies that those who do not agree with them are advocating suppression of women's rights.

Words and images are frequently used to create emotional effects. For example, pro-life advocates use the word "baby" to describe all stages of development in a pregnancy. They frequently call women who choose abortions and doctors who perform them "baby killers." To spread the antiabortion message, bloody pictures of aborted fetuses give the impression that all abortions result in babies hacked to pieces.

Pro-choice advocates are selective in their language also. For example, they usually use the word "embryo," "fetus," or other medical term to refer to stages of a pregnancy. Frequently the pro-choice message is accompanied by pictures of back alleys, dirty restrooms, and dead women to warn that if abortions become illegal they will take place under unsavory and life-threatening conditions.

Personhood

Abortion arguments often originate because of conflicting ideas about "personhood" when life begins and a fetus becomes a person. In general there are two sides. According to one view, human life begins at conception—the moment the female ovum is fertilized by the male sperm to form a zygote, or single-celled organism. From conception on, a human is developing, thus abortion at any point in a pregnancy is akin to murder, this argument says. Some even declare that using contraceptives is a "murderous act" because birth control prevents a sperm from fertilizing an egg.

Those on the other side of the argument acknowledge that the egg and sperm have the potential to become full human persons. But, they say, every month girls and women who menstruate lose eggs in the menstrual blood flow. Boys and men release millions of sperm when they masturbate or have wet dreams. So should all of the lost eggs and sperm be considered potential persons? Even if an egg is fertilized, that does not mean that a zygote, embryo, or fetus has the same value or rights as a living person,

Demonstrators in front of the Supreme Court building express strong feelings about their side of the abortion debate.

say opponents of fetal personhood. They contend that personhood is achieved at birth.

Concepts of personhood stem from social customs, religious beliefs, and medical and scientific findings as well as legal decisions. In some countries, for example, an infant is not considered a person until she or he is named, which could be days or months after birth.

Religious doctrines enter into arguments for or against personhood. In Jewish law, for instance, a fetus "becomes a full-fledged human being when the head emerges from the womb. . . . In the case of a 'feet-first' delivery, it happens when most of the fetal body is outside the mother's body."[3]

To support the view that life begins at conception, Roman Catholics and evangelical Protestants are just two groups that cite biblical verses as proof of their belief. They declare that any harm to the fetus is immoral and should be illegal. Yet other religious groups, such as Reform and Conservative Jews, Unitarians, and some mainstream Protestant denominations, insist that biblical codes on reproductive matters are not clear-cut and are open to personal interpretations. They view the morality of abortion in light of a woman's circumstances at the time, taking into consideration the quality of her life and that of her potential child.

Scientists also have diverse opinions on the question of personhood, particularly as they have gained more knowledge about the fetus. Some medical researchers assert that because a zygote contains the genetic material to create a human life—a distinct entity—that entity should be treated as a potential person with legal protections. In addition, with advances in medical technology and the ability to keep premature babies alive (some born as early as twenty to twenty-four weeks of gestation), questions about when a fetus is viable and a person become more complex.

Researchers on the other side claim that without a functioning brain, a person does not exist. According to their reasoning, a fetus may have brain waves, or electrical activity, but the brain waves are not meaningful until the whole brain begins to take shape (about the seventh month of pregnancy). According to the late Carl Sagan, Pulitzer Prize winner and noted science writer:

> Brain wave patterns typical of adult human brains do not appear in the fetus until about the 30th week of pregnancy. Fetuses younger than this—however alive and active they may be—lack the necessary brain architecture. They cannot yet think.[4]

In short, the brain is the most complex part of the human body, and all parts of the brain must develop and work together—including the 100 billion neurons, or nerve cells, and billions of dendrites and axons, extensions that transmit messages to and from neurons—so that a person can think and function.[5]

Fetal Protection

In early 2002, a change in a federal regulation sparked even more debate on abortion and the concept of personhood. The U.S. Department of Health and Human Services (HHS) announced that it was changing the way it classified children who were eligible for health care funded by the federal government. As the law was written, those eligible for such health care were individuals under age nineteen.

With the rule change, states can provide health care from the time of conception, classifying a fetus as an "unborn child." Those who supported this classification include Tommy Thompson, Secretary of HHS, and President George W. Bush, both of whom oppose abortion. Along with other Bush administration supporters, they argued that the change would provide prenatal health care for women who otherwise would not qualify for it. Opponents say that prenatal care could have been provided through programs that already exist for pregnant women without changing the status of the fetus. The status change, they contend, is part of an antiabortion agenda.

Pro-choice advocates assert that other efforts are under way to establish the fetus as a person, such as the Unborn Victims of Violence Act, which the U.S. House of Representatives passed in 2001. It has not been approved by the Senate, however. If enacted, the federal criminal code would be amended to create a separate offense for someone who causes the death of, or bodily injury to, a fetus, or as the wording of the bills states, an "unborn child." In the view of the Religious Coalition for Reproductive Choice,

> This bill would, for the first time under federal law, recognize a zygote (fertilized egg), blastocyst (preimplantation embryo), embryo, or fetus as a "person," with rights separate from and equal to those of a woman and would deem those rights to be worthy of legal protection. . . .
>
> The Unborn Victims of Violence Act would adopt one religious belief about the beginning of life—that the fetus at all stages of development is a person—and make it the law for all, regardless of individual beliefs. As an interfaith coalition, we point out that government must not legislate, and thus impose, one religious view about the beginning of life on all people.[6]

About half the states already have what are often called "unborn victim laws." In those states, if a pregnant woman and the fetus are killed in a car accident or because of an assault, the person causing the woman's death can also be charged with the death of her "unborn child." By using the term "unborn child," opponents argue, the laws establish a fetus as a person before birth. However, these laws usually exempt abortion, which raises questions: Is a fetus a person in "unborn victim laws" but not considered a person when the abortion exemption is applied? How can a fetus be a victim in one case and not another? Are "unborn victim laws" designed to elevate the status of a fetus and make the pregnant woman nothing more than a fetal container or incubator?

Fetal protection controversies also focus on possible health hazards to the fetus *in utero* (in the womb), and some legal and medical experts believe that pregnant women who do not follow established medical advice to protect their fetuses should be held legally responsible—prosecuted for fetal abuse—if negligent acts harm or injure a fetus. In some cases, pregnant girls and women are forced against their wishes or religious beliefs to undergo various medical treatments or even surgery in order to protect the well-being of the fetus.

One well-publicized case in the late 1980s involved twenty-seven-year-old Angela Carder, who previously had had bouts with cancer. When she learned that the disease was in remission, she married and became pregnant. When she was twenty-six weeks pregnant, the cancer returned. As her condition became worse, she entered the George Washington University Medical Center in Washington, D.C. There Carder, her husband, parents, and the doctors "agreed on a course of treatment aimed at keeping her alive for at least another two weeks, at which point intervention to save the fetus might be possible," the ACLU reported.

However, Carder's condition deteriorated rapidly, and the hospital's administration was afraid that she would not survive for two weeks. Lawyers for the hospital went to court, and a judge authorized the hospital to perform an immediate cesarean section.

But the surgery was against the wishes of Carder's husband, parents, and obstetricians, all of whom feared that neither Angela Carder nor the fetus would survive the surgery. Her cancer specialist was not consulted; he said later that he would have opposed the cesarean section. When Angela Carder found out about the court order, she said several times, "I don't want it done."[7]

The ACLU on behalf of the family tried to get the D.C. Court of Appeals to block the order. But the court refused and the surgery proceeded. The premature baby died within two hours, and Carder died two days later.

The ACLU—joined by the American Medical Association and various religious, women's, and civil rights groups—went to the appeals court again, asking the court to issue an opinion and vacate (set aside) the order for a forced C-section. This time, the court ruled that Angela Carder's right to make an informed decision about medical treatment had been violated. According to the ACLU,

> When an attorney for the hospital argued that it was appropriate to sacrifice a dying woman for her fetus, one judge replied incredulously, "Are you

urging this court to find that you can handcuff a woman to a bed and force her to give birth?" . . . The court resoundingly concluded that in virtually all circumstances a woman—not doctors or a judge—should make medical decisions on behalf of herself and her fetus.[8]

As a result of the court ruling, the George Washington University Medical Center agreed to respect patients' decisions even when they went against medical advice.

Regardless of the ruling in the Carder case, other court-ordered cesareans have taken place in hospitals across the United States. Pregnant women have also been forced to undergo medical treatments that go against their religious beliefs—for instance, blood transfusions, which are not permitted by Jehovah's Witnesses. Some pregnant women have been jailed because they have not sought prenatal care. In a Wisconsin case, for example, law enforcement officials held a pregnant sixteen-year-old in detention, claiming that she was a runaway and would not get the medical care need to protect her fetus.

"Pregnancy Police"

Over the past few decades, people nationwide have been concerned about alcohol and other drug abuse, which has prompted numerous national and state efforts to combat this problem. Some of the efforts have been directed toward pregnant women because of health risks to the fetus. For example, when a pregnant woman drinks alcohol, the fetus she carries risks fetal alcohol syndrome (FAS), a disorder that can result in lifelong consequences. Children with FAS may suffer mental retardation, stunted growth, learning disabilities, and serious behavioral problems.

A pregnant woman with a substance abuse problem can also seriously harm her fetus, sometimes causing a baby to be born addicted to drugs. Developmental and behavior problems may also occur in children whose mothers were addicted to drugs when they were pregnant.

Some states have attempted to protect the fetus by passing laws that make drug use by a pregnant woman a form of child abuse. Critics of such laws say that punishing pregnant women is not the answer. They believe that funds to treat drug addiction, which are in short supply in many states, should be increased instead. Critics also charge that the "pregnancy police" are more concerned about a fetus than an addicted woman.

The Alan Guttmacher Institute reports that pregnant women who have used drugs, particularly cocaine, have been

> arrested and charged with a wide range of crimes, including possession of a controlled substance, delivering drugs to a minor (through the umbilical cord), corruption of a minor, and child abuse and neglect. Others have been charged with assault with a deadly weapon and manslaughter.[9]

In 1989, local law officials and the public hospital in Charleston, South Carolina, had a policy of testing pregnant women for drug abuse without their consent. Women were subject to testing if they had a history of drug or alcohol abuse, obtained minimal or no prenatal care, experienced unexplained preterm labor, or had a child with birth defects. According to the ACLU:

> In the early months of the program, women were immediately arrested after they or their newborns tested positive for cocaine. One woman spent the last three weeks of her pregnancy in jail. During this time she received prenatal care in handcuffs and shackles. Authorities arrested another woman soon after she gave birth; still bleeding and dressed in only a hospital gown, she was handcuffed and taken to the city jail.[10]

The Charleston policy was changed in 1990 to allow pregnant women who used drugs to go to a treatment center instead of prison. However, the ACLU appealed one case to the U.S. Supreme Court (*Ferguson* v. *City of Charleston, South Carolina*), and in March 2001, the Court ruled that the hospital policy violated the Fourth Amendment to the U.S. Constitution, which protects citizens against unreasonable searches. Catherine Weiss, director of the ACLU's Reproductive Freedom Project, said the decision made clear that women

Some women use harmful substances such as alcohol and tobacco during pregnancy. Some people have proposed laws that make this a form of child abuse.

do not "become wards of the state or forfeit their constitutional rights" when they become pregnant.[11]

More State Laws

Along with fetal personhood and protection debates are controversies over a variety of other state laws that place restrictions on abortion. Laws restricting intact dilation and extraction, or D&X, are examples. State laws or proposed laws are patterned after a 1995 federal bill known as the Partial-Birth Abortion Ban Act, which was reintroduced several times and in 2003 was passed by the U.S. Congress. The ACLU immediately denounced the ban and filed a lawsuit charging that it "callously disregards women's health in pursuit of an extreme anti-choice agenda."

In the view of the ACLU, the passage of the act is no different from a Nebraska law struck down by the Supreme Court. That law made it a criminal offense with a sentence of up to twenty years for any doctor who performed a D&X procedure, unless a woman's life was in danger. No exception was made for the health of a pregnant woman, and the law was found unconstitutional. At least thirty other states have attempted to pass D&X bans since 1995, but in states where those laws have been challenged, "the courts have declared the laws unconstitutional and blocked enforcement," the ACLU reported.[12]

More than forty states have passed laws requiring a minor (in most states, someone under the age of eighteen) to obtain parental consent or to notify a parent or both parents before having an abortion. In a few states, grandparents or other adult relatives can be involved instead of parents. Some states allow an exception if a judge determines that parental involvement would endanger the minor or if there is an emergency situation.[13] However, some of these laws have been challenged in court and have been declared invalid or have not been strictly enforced.

Those who support such laws insist that involving parents in abortion decisions is an important aspect of good family relationships—young women need the support and guidance of parents or other family members. The laws, advocates argue, alert parents to possible physical and emotional dangers their daughters might face. They also contend that states with parental consent laws have seen teenage pregnancy rates as well as abortion rates decrease. In addition, supporters point out that parents are legally responsible for the care of their children and that they must sign consent forms for much less serious procedures—for instance, if their daughter wants to take an aspirin or get her ears pierced.

According to *The Abortion Resource Handbook,* approximately half of pregnant teenagers discuss their abortion decision with their parents, whether they live in a state with a parental involvement law or not.[14] Some teenagers who have notified their parents have found them supportive, and sometimes the experience brings them closer together.

Parental consent and notification laws, however, have been widely criticized by those who believe many teenagers will be physically or emotionally abused if they tell their parents about their pregnancies. The laws may also prevent a teenager from getting an abortion or may delay an abortion until a later, more dangerous time in the pregnancy, opponents say.

Opponents of parental consent laws also say that teenagers are concerned that their parents will no longer love or respect them. The story of Becky Bell of Indiana is often told to bolster this argument. Becky lived near Indianapolis, and in 1988 she was a junior in high school when she got pregnant. She tried to get an abortion at a health clinic, but Indiana law requires parental consent. Because she was afraid to disappoint her parents, she got an illegal abortion. She died a week later of complications from the abortion.

Becky Bell's parents, who once championed parental consent laws, now insist that parental involvement laws seriously endanger the very families and teenagers they are intended to protect. As Becky's father, quoted in *Scholastic Update,* noted: "My daughter was denied the right to make a safe and reasonable choice on her own."[15] Becky's mother said that her daughter died of an infection which literally destroyed her lungs. According to the coroner's report; the infection was due to "an illegal, botched abortion; dirty instruments had been used."[16]

A number of pro-life organizations have disputed the report that Becky Bell died due to a botched abortion. One organization, Feminists for Life of America (FFL), contends, "Strong evidence is accumulating that Rebecca Bell had no abortion at all," and was likely pregnant, developed pneumonia, and had begun to have a miscarriage before she went to the hospital. In the opinion of FFL, "parental involvement would have saved Becky's life; if the law had worked, and she had talked to her parents, they could have treated the pneumonia in time." FFL acknowledges that teenagers—even those who have good family relationships—are fearful of telling their parents about a pregnancy. But, FFL states, this is not

> an argument against the law; for the teen's sake, the parents have the right and obligation to assist in such momentous health-care situations. Most girls will do what they always have—take a deep breath and go ahead and tell their parents.[17]

The American Association of University Women (AAUW) has weighed in on this subject, declaring:

> Mandatory parental involvement in reproductive health services, including family planning and abortion, often causes minors to skip or postpone needed medical care. Because pregnancy rates and sexually transmitted disease (STD) infection rates among minors remain unacceptably high, we must ensure confidential access to abortion, family planning, and other basic health care services for those young people who are unable or afraid to speak to a parent about these issues.[18]

While doctors generally counsel teenagers to talk to their parents about an abortion and provide minors with information about their options, physicians are aware that pregnant teenagers can have serious concerns about parental involvement. The Council on Ethical and Judicial Affairs of the American Medical Association (AMA) adopted a policy in 1993 that says that physicians should know the law in their state and "ensure that their procedures are consistent with their legal obligations." But the AMA policy also states:

> The patient—even an adolescent—generally must decide whether, on balance, parental involvement is advisable. Accordingly, minors should ultimately be allowed to decide whether parental involvement is appropriate.[19]

The AMA Council stressed that a minor's need for privacy may be so great that she would run away from home or have an illegal or self-induced abortion.[20]

Debates over parental involvement laws are likely to continue, as will controversies over other abortion issues. Because these arguments are frequently framed as pro-life or pro-choice, each position is treated separately in the next two chapters: first the pro-life view and then the pro-choice view.

5

The Pro-Life View

Abortion is murder, plain and simple.
Babies are being butchered.
It's a child, not a choice!

These are just a few of the statements, sometimes used as slogans, by some members of the pro-life movement. Those who call themselves pro-life are people from varied backgrounds and age groups. High school and college students; doctors, nurses, and other health-care providers; politicians; lawyers; Americans of varied ethnic groups and economic status; religious and nonreligious are among those who have pro-life beliefs.

What is a pro-life belief? What does "pro-life" mean? In the early 1970s when the pro-life movement began, most "pro-lifers" opposed abortion no matter what the circumstances of the pregnant woman. During the next decade, some pro-life advocates made exceptions for women whose lives were at risk if they continued their pregnancies and for victims of rape and incest. By the 1990s, some people (politicians especially) began calling themselves pro-life even if their only opposition to abortion was to the D&X procedure.[1]

In short, there is no exact definition today for the term "pro-life." Most people who call themselves pro-choice also say they are pro-life, that is, *for* life. But in the context of abortion, many pro-life supporters repeatedly argue: Human life begins at conception and should be legally protected—that is, they should have a right to life.

The concept of a right to life became the name for the National Right to Life Committee (NRLC). This organization was formed in 1973, not long after the *Roe* v. *Wade* decision. Nearly all states have pro-life organizations, and local pro-life groups have formed as well. In addition, there are numerous pro-life organizations on college campuses, from American Collegians for Life to Xavier University Students for Life.

Other national organizations, such as Americans United For Life, Feminists for Life, and National Coalition for Life and Peace, have been established. Some other pro-life groups include Life Athletes, the National Memorial for the Unborn, Black Americans for Life, Pro-Life Alliance of Gays and Lesbians,

Atheist and Agnostic Pro-Life League, Rightgrrl, and Women Affirming Life.

Many people with pro-life views base their beliefs on religious doctrine. For example, according to Islamic teachings,

> The right to life is God-given. NO human should take away that right. The general rule, therefore, is that abortion is not permitted in Islam.
>
> However, Islam is a very practical religion. It includes principles to deal with exceptional cases. One such principle is that when the pregnancy threatens the life of the mother, an abortion may be performed. Although the lives of both mother and child are sacred, in this case it is better to save the principal life, the life of the mother. Even in this case, it would be better if the abortion is done before the foetus is 120 days old, for that is when the soul is breathed into the foetus.
>
> Islam does not permit abortion in other cases.[2]

Those who follow current Roman Catholic teachings generally oppose abortion, although individuals and groups such as Catholics for a Free Choice disagree with the church's stand. Fundamentalist Protestant churches and other religious organizations—Orthodox Jews, for example— also have doctrines opposing all abortions except to save the life of a pregnant woman.

In addition, nonreligious individuals and groups have pro-life views. Consider Nat Hentoff, a well-known columnist and a former pro-choice advocate who now describes himself as a "Jewish, atheist, civil libertarian, left-wing pro-lifer." He writes that being without theology isn't the slightest hindrance to being pro-life. As any obstetrics manual . . . points out, there are two patients involved, and the one not yet born "should be given the same meticulous care by the physician that we long have given the pregnant woman." Nor, biologically, does it make any sense to draw life-or-death lines at viability. Once implantation takes place, this being has all the genetic information within that makes each human being unique. And he or she embodies continually developing human life from that point on. It misses a crucial point to say that the extermination can take place because the brain has not yet functioned or because that thing is not yet a "person." Whether the life is cut off in the fourth week or the fourteenth, the victim is one of our species, and has been from the start.[3]

Pro-life organizations that are nonsectarian—that is, not affiliated with a particular religious group—frequently base their arguments on the belief that abortion is wrong because it ignores the basic value of any form of human life. For example, Pagans for Life argue "all living things are deserving of respect and a life free of abuse." Modern pagans basically believe in individual spiritual growth that is in harmony with the earth. In their view,

> every living human being, born or pre-born, has certain inherent human rights. These rights include the right to keep one's own life and to live free from abuse. Children, born and pre-born, and those who are dependent on others due to age or disability, have the right to adequate and compassionate care. Abortion, like any form of violence against a child, is a violation of the most basic of human rights.[4]

Many abortion opponents base their position on religious beliefs. These students have set up a display of crosses on the school lawn; each cross represents one of the abortions performed each day in the United States.

Feminists for Life of America, another nonsectarian group, opposes abortion because they see it as a form of violence and exploitation of women. FFL works in the tradition of nineteenth-century feminists to improve the status of women, which, the organization believes, will eliminate the need for abortions.

Other nonsectarian groups include Americans United for Life (AUL), a public-interest law firm based in Chicago, Illinois. AUL declares that it "has led the way in the effort to restore the sanctity of human life in American law and culture. AUL defends human life in the courts, in state legislatures, in Congress, and through public education."[5] One other group, Life

Athletes, is a coalition of Olympic and professional athletes who say they are "committed to leading lives of virtue, abstinence, and respect for life."[6] Another is the Pro-Life Alliance of Gays and Lesbians, who are "committed to raising awareness of the pro-life ethic as consistent with the gay and lesbian struggle for human rights." Their message: "Human rights start when human life begins!"[7]

The Adoption Option

Those who oppose abortion often advocate that a pregnant woman continue her pregnancy and then release the baby for adoption. How do birth mothers feel when they place a child for adoption? They often express great sadness during the time before and after they deliver a child. But many also believe they have made the right choice and are thankful that there are adoptive parents eagerly willing to make their children part of their families.

Yet placing a child for adoption can have drawbacks and may create traumas. The adoption process may not succeed because of legal problems or because a child is born with health risks. In some cases, a baby's father or grandparents may object to adoption, or the birth mother may decide that she wants her child returned after the baby has been placed in another home.

It is not unusual for mothers who place their babies for adoption to feel a sense of loss, grief, anger, or even relief. Counselors at family service agencies and crisis pregnancy centers can help women deal with their feelings.

Pregnancy Centers

In recent years pro-life groups have set up emergency pregnancy centers that usually advertise as facilities that primarily provide assistance, counseling, and information on alternatives to abortion. These centers may offer free pregnancy testing, ultrasound tests, education regarding sexual abstinence, and adoption information. Some provide housing—maternity homes—for women who carry their pregnancies to term. Many also supply maternity items and baby clothing, diapers, formula, and cribs. Parenting classes in several languages may also be offered.

The pregnancy centers are supported by private donations or religious groups. Center counselors usually explain fetal development to pregnant women, using medical pictures or models. Counselors focus on both the physical risks and the emotional difficulties a woman may face if she chooses abortion, and they emphasize that no one can force her to have an abortion. The centers also provide information on support groups or counseling for women who have had abortions.

Pro-Life Activists

A 2002 Gallup Poll found that among all Americans, only a minority are "highly motivated on the abortion issue." Within that minority, "the pro-life side has the edge, as those opposed to abortion tend to feel more

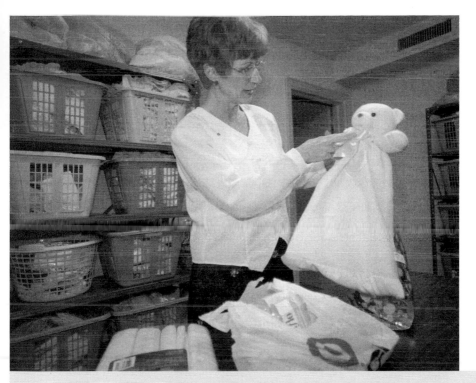

Crisis pregnancy centers usually offer alternatives to abortion; many of them also offer support to pregnant women. Above, a center in Charlotte, N.C., has collected supplies for mothers and babies.

strongly about their position and are more likely to base their vote choices on it than are those in favor of abortion rights," the poll said.[8]

Supporting political candidates who oppose abortion is an important part of pro-life activities. Pro-life activists often lobby U.S. senators and representatives and state legislators on behalf of their cause, as do many on the other side of the issue.

Many people who share pro-life beliefs become part of right-to-life groups. One such activist is Derrick Jones, a youth outreach coordinator for NRLC. He spent most of his growing-up years helping his grandmother with pro-life activities, from stuffing envelopes for political campaigns to going door-to-door handing out literature. He became involved in Teens for Life in high school, then College Students for Life when he was a student at Catholic University of America in Washington, D.C. He now works in the pro-life movement.[9]

Many in the pro-life movement feel very strongly about spreading their antiabortion message. How is that done? It might be a simple act, one that is popular with teenagers: wearing a T-shirt that says "Abortion is mean."[10] Or it could be taking part in the annual "March for Life" in Washington, D.C., to protest the Supreme Court decision in *Roe* v. *Wade*.

In numerous states, activists are working to get legislatures to pass laws allowing specialty license plates that say, "Choose Life." The phrase adopts the argument often used by those on the pro-choice side who advocate a woman's right to choose abortion. The profit from the specialty plates—which cost about $20 more than regular license plates—goes to pro-life groups for such activities as running crisis pregnancy centers.

Laws in six states—Alabama, Florida, Louisiana, Mississippi, Oklahoma, and South Carolina—have been passed to make "Choose Life" license plates available. Similar legislation is pending in at least twelve other states—California, Illinois, Iowa,

This is the type of license plate proposed to the Florida legislature that promotes the pro-life viewpoint.

Kansas, Kentucky, Michigan, Minnesota, North Carolina, Ohio, Pennsylvania, South Carolina, and West Virginia. Florida is the only state selling "Choose Life" specialty plates, although the practice has been challenged as unconstitutional in that state because it presents only the pro-life viewpoint in the abortion debate.

In late December 2002, the U.S. District Court in South Carolina found the plates unconstitutional because no pro-choice license plates have been allowed. The court held that this violates free-speech rights and is discriminatory. The state will appeal, and the case could be heard by the U.S. Supreme Court.

One of the most common pro-life activities all over the United States is demonstrating at abortion clinics.

Some activists demonstrate on a regular basis, as this Internet announcement from Pennsylvania reveals:

> We are Berks County pro-lifers. Many of us gather every Thursday morning in front of Planned Parenthood . . . in Reading [Pennsylvania]. Planned Parenthood is the only child-killing organization in Berks County and the largest one in the world. Please join us Thursday mornings, for four minutes to four hours, because that is when the abortionist from Bucks County . . . comes here to kill our babies.[11]

What do pro-lifers do at a clinic protest? Some hand out antiabortion pamphlets or carry signs with pictures of bloody aborted fetuses and messages such as "Our Laws Are Evil. Babies Are Being Butchered!!" Others try to block clinic entrances and convince pregnant women that they should not have an abortion.

Not all protests are held at clinics, however. In numerous cases, protesters have picketed homes of clinic doctors and workers. Demonstrations are also held on busy street corners and at large public events around the nation.

Antiabortion Extremists

Most pro-life groups conduct peaceful demonstrations to oppose abortion and lobby for antiabortion laws. They may practice civil disobedience in some demonstrations—refusing police orders to disburse, for example, which may result in arrests—but they denounce violence. Yet some groups and individuals advocate and practice violence to spread their

Some antiabortion activists have protested with peaceful civil disobedience. Here a demonstrator is arrested after trying to block a clinic entrance.

antiabortion messages. Such extremists believe that assaults, from kidnapping to murder, are justifiable because they are preventing death from abortions.

During the 1990s, extremists were responsible for dozens of clinic arsons and bombings and at least one hundred attacks using butyric acid, a liquid that can harm people and damage buildings with a foul-smelling odor that is difficult to remove. They have also murdered seven people and attempted to murder more than a dozen others working in abortion clinics in the United States and Canada.[12]

One of the first to be killed during the 1990s was abortion doctor David Gunn of Florida. He was shot in 1993 by Michael Griffin, who claimed he acted in the name of God. His work was praised by other extremists, such as Shelly Shannon, who followed the teachings of the Army of God, a right-wing extremist group. Shannon had committed herself to violence and engaged in a year-long spree of arson and butyric acid attacks across three states in 1992. In 1993 she shot George Tiller, a Kansas doctor who performed abortions. Tiller was not seriously wounded. Shannon was arrested, convicted of attempted murder, and sentenced to prison.

A few days after the shooting, she wrote,

> I'm not denying I shot Tiller. But I deny that it was wrong. It was the most holy, most righteous thing I've ever done. I have no regrets. I hope he's not killing babies today. If he is, at least I tried.[13]

Another victim of pro-life extremists was Dr. Barnett Slepian of Amherst, New York, shot to death in his home by a sniper in 1998. James Kopp, the man charged with the murder of Slepian, was captured in France in March 2001, after more than two years running from police. Kopp is also suspected in four other shootings of abortion providers (none were fatal), and in 2002 was returned to the United States to stand trial. In 2003, he was convicted of second-degree murder but expressed no remorse for assassinating Slepian.

Although violence seemed to decrease somewhat in 2000, incidents increased the following year, due primarily to anthrax threats. In 2001, hundreds of letters were sent out to abortion providers across the United States threatening them with the deadly anthrax bacteria. Dozens of such threats had occurred in previous years, but letters claiming to contain anthrax intensified after the terrorist attacks on the World Trade Center and the Pentagon and anthrax deaths in 2001. No anthrax was found in the letters, but some contained an insecticide that at first tested positive for anthrax.

Clayton Lee Waagner, accused of sending about three hundred anthrax threat letters and posting threats on Web sites to kill people working at abortion clinics, was apprehended in Cincinnati, Ohio, in November 2001. According to his testimony, he claimed God had "anointed" him to be a one-man terrorist against the abortion industry. He had hoped to kill an abortion doctor because, as he told investigators, "I don't like these people at all. I hate what they do."[14]

Extremists also have supported a Web site known as the Nuremberg Files, which has equated abortion with the crimes of World War II Nazis who were tried at Nuremberg, Germany. Neal Horsley set up the site, which encourages "concerned citizens" to collect information on abortionists and those who support them, including photos and videotapes of their homes, family members, cars, license plate numbers, social security numbers, and much more so that, as Horsley's Web site states, "one day we may be able to hold them on trial for crimes against humanity."[15]

When the site was first posted, it contained western-style "Wanted" posters and listed names, addresses, phone numbers, and a great deal of other personal information about people who perform abortions. Names of people who had been murdered because of their abortion activities appeared with slashes through them. About two dozen servers refused to host the site, but it was difficult to remove it from the Internet altogether because of free speech rights.

In June 2002, the Ninth U.S. Circuit Court of Appeals ruled, in *Planned Parenthood* v. *American Coalition of Life Activists,* that it was illegal for Horsley to post crossed-out names of murdered abortionists and western-style "Wanted" posters with the names of abortion doctors. But Horsley continues to post the list of names in another format. In addition, the site posts photographs of what Horsley calls "homicidal mothers" taken by activists who wait outside clinics to videotape patients entering the facilities. He also plans a lawsuit "to have our right to publish factually verifiable information about the terror of legalized abortion restored."[16]

Some Other Pro-Life Issues

Rather than engage in extremist actions, most pro-life activities are focused on making political and social changes. In fact, in recent years, pro-life groups have emphasized issues that they believe are related to their antiabortion efforts. One of the issues is in vitro fertilization (IVF), a common method used to help women become pregnant when they are unable to conceive. In this medical procedure, a woman takes hormones to stimulate the production of multiple ova, or egg cells. Then a doctor extracts the eggs, places them in a petri dish along with the sperm of the woman's partner or other donor. The fertilized eggs (zygotes) are placed in an incubator. Within a few days, after the cells divide, several embryos are implanted in the woman's uterus. Embryos that are "left over" may be frozen so that if the woman does not become pregnant, she can try again. Or the embryos are discarded or used for research.

In the pro-life view, which says that personhood begins at conception, destroying an embryo is killing a person. The pro-life organization American Life League contends that in vitro fertilization has led to human embryonic stem-cell research and eventually will lead to human cloning.[17] In fact, some individuals claimed in 2002 that they had produced humans from cloned embryos, although this has yet to be proven.

The issue of cloning for the purpose of harvesting embryonic stem cells has created widespread controversy; it has been the subject of numerous articles and books, and space does not permit broad coverage here. But briefly, cloning human embryos today is the process of developing replicas so that they can be used for research. This therapeutic cloning, as it is called, is meant to prevent and treat major diseases and ailments. As with cells derived from leftover embryos, tissues from cloned embryos, which are destroyed in the process, are basic cells that can be grown in laboratories and develop into nerve, muscle, liver, and other specialized cells. These cells then can be implanted in a person with a serious illness. Scientists say the tissue will develop healthy cells to cure ailments such as diabetes, heart damage, Parkinson's disease and other nerve disorders, and countless other ills. According to researchers at the University of Wisconsin at Madison, "Replacing faulty cells with healthy ones offers hope of lifelong treatment. Similarly, failing hearts and other organs, in theory, could be shored up by injecting healthy cells to replace damaged or diseased cells."[18]

Many pro-life activists (as well as some people who do not share pro-life views) have urged legislators to oppose government support for embryonic stem-cell research and cloning embryos to create stem cells. Indeed, in August 2001, President George W. Bush banned the use of federal money to create embryos for research but allowed government funds to be used to study embryonic stem cells that have previously been taken from frozen embryos at fertility clinics.[19]

Numerous pro-lifers believe that even though someone might benefit from embryonic stem cells, using them does not justify "taking a life" and destroying embryos for experiments. This issue has divided some in the pro-life movement. For example, Senator Orrin Hatch of Utah, who has been a staunch antiabortionist for many years, supports a federal bill that would allow embryo cloning for research, or therapeutic cloning. In Hatch's view, "a critical part of being pro-life is to support measures that help the living."[20]

Stem Cells

The National Institutes of Health developed a primer on stem cells to answer such questions as: What are stem cells? What different types of stem cells are there and where do they come from? What is the potential for new medical treatments using stem cells? What research is needed to make such treatments a reality? Some excerpts are below.

> Stem cells . . . are unspecialized cells that . . . can be induced to become cells with special functions. . . .
>
> In the 3 to 5 day old embryo, . . . a small group of about 30 cells . . . gives rise to the hundreds of highly specialized cells needed to make up an adult organism. In the developing fetus, stem cells in developing tissues give rise to the multiple specialized cell types that make up the heart, lung, skin, and other tissues. In some adult tissues . . . stem cells generate replacements for cells that are lost through normal wear and tear, injury, or disease.
>
> Embryonic stem cells . . . are derived from embryos that develop from eggs that have been fertilized in vitro . . . and then donated for research purposes with informed consent of the donors. They are not derived from eggs fertilized in a woman's body.[21]

Hatch's stance on human cloning research has angered some pro-life advocates such as the group Concerned Women for America (CWA). They have lobbied for a bill, supported by President Bush, that bans all human cloning. In February 2003, Sandy Rios, president of CWA, signed "The Sanctity of Life in a Brave New World: A Manifesto on Biotechnology and Human Dignity," along with other pro-life leaders. The CWA declared that this outlines a basic moral framework for decision making in this emerging field. "We know that Congress has the duty, and we believe Congress has the will to regulate biotechnology so that the industry will not be permitted to sacrifice one life for the convenience or well-being of another," said Rios. She noted:

> I am particularly concerned with the burdens of cloning that women will be forced to bear. Cloning requires enormous amounts of eggs to be harvested from women. Further, the method of cultivating these eggs poses life-threatening risks. Even the language used to describe the process shows that science views women more as a crop in a farmer's field than as human beings endowed with inalienable rights.[22]

While embryo research is an issue within the pro-life movement, it is only part of their basic concerns: to ensure the sanctity of life, defend all life, and restrict abortions by law. To that end, the pro-life movement will certainly continue to counter pro-choice views.

The Pro-Choice View

Abortion rights are pro-life.
Get your laws off my body.
Every mother willing—every child wanted.

Like pro-lifers, those who advocate the
pro-choice view make diverse statements
about abortion and use slogans to advance
their stand. Also like antiabortionists, pro-
choice advocates are people from varied
backgrounds and age groups. Students in
high school and college students; a variety
of health-care providers; professionals in
politics, law, and many other fields; Americans of varied ethnic and socioeconomic
status; members of religious groups and the

nonreligious are among those who call themselves pro-choice.

What does pro-choice mean? For some it means that "women are autonomous beings with the brains and the right to make their own decisions about their lives."[1] Or as the Pro-Choice Public Education Project puts it: "It's pro-choice or no choice."[2]

Kate Michelman, president of NARAL: Pro-Choice America (formerly the National Abortion and Reproductive Rights Action League), explained: "We are Pro-Choice America because that name reflects the fundamental question our movement asks—the question of choice—the question of: Who decides? Women or politicians?"[3]

The Republican Pro-Choice Coalition posts this on its Web site:

> Traditional Republican philosophy argues for less government interference in all aspects of Americans' lives, on the theory that individuals make better decisions than do governments. Similarly, a person who is pro-choice believes that government should not dictate reproductive health decisions. The pro-choice position neither advocates for or against abortions, instead, simply advocates that government should not interfere in such decisions that are best left to individuals.[4]

Personal Views

For teenagers and women who have had abortions, the meaning of pro-choice is reflected in the reasons they chose to end their pregnancies. Some say they do not want to have children if they are unable to care for them or if the father refuses to accept responsibility for his child's care. Many young people are concerned about their own life circumstances and their ability to raise children. Others, who have considered adoption as an option, contend they could not go through with a pregnancy for nine months and then give a child away.

Kate Michelman has frequently expressed her personal views regarding abortions. She is dedicated to protecting women's right to choose because of her own experience. In 1970, she had an abortion. But first she was required to get permission from her husband, who had deserted the family. Then she had to face a hospital panel made up entirely of men, who questioned her about her decision. She was devastated, but as she told a Chicago reporter, her "family's survival was at stake. For me it was a difficult choice. But it was mine alone to make."[5]

Maureen Britell, executive director of Voters for Choice, has a similar view. In 1994, she and her husband had a daughter, Samantha, and were expecting a much-wanted second child. Then, twenty weeks into the pregnancy, they learned that the fetus was anencephalic; it could not survive outside the womb. Years later, on the PBS program *Now* with Bill Moyers, she explained:

> We decided to end the pregnancy because it was condemning me to a death watch, which made no sense to me as a mom for Samantha, to me as a wife, to me as a mom of the baby I was carrying. It just sounded so cruel.[6]

Kate Michelman is president of NARAL: Pro-Choice America—
formerly the National Abortion and Reproductive Rights Action
League. Like many women who have had experience with
abortion, Michelman opposes restrictions on the procedure
for others.

Pro-Choice and Religion

Many religious groups and individuals believe that a
woman's right to an abortion is a moral choice and
a private matter. The interfaith Religious Coalition
for Reproductive Choice (RCRC), which includes
more than forty national organizations from eighteen
denominations, movements, and faith groups, stated
their position:

> Coalition members hold in high respect the value of
> potential human life, while remaining committed to

women as responsible, moral decision-makers. The coalition encourages decisions concerning a problem pregnancy to be made in consultation with families, clergy, and doctors. The Religious Coalition opposes any attempt to enact into secular law restrictions on reproductive choice based on one particular theological definition of when a fetus becomes a human being.[7]

According to Southern Baptist theologian Dr. Paul D. Simmons, "The claim that the Bible teaches that the fetus is a person from the moment of conception is problematic at best. Such a judgment rests on subjective and personal factors, not explicit biblical teachings."[8]

Many religious groups and individuals strongly disagree with those who claim there are biblical bans against abortion. Pro-choice religious people find no condemnations of abortion in the Bible. And many believe that it is up to the individual and his or her conscience to determine whether abortion is or is not sinful or immoral.

That view is shared by some Catholics who disagree with their church's stand against all abortions. As Frances Kissling, president of Catholics for a Free Choice, wrote:

> Pro-choice is not pro-abortion. Pro-choice people have many different beliefs about the morality of abortion. For some it is almost never morally justified; for others it is often justified. What they agree on is that each woman must weigh her beliefs and circumstances without interference by the state and make her own decision. Four hundred thousand U.S. Catholic women weigh

The Reverend Katherine Hancock Ragsdale, an Episcopal priest, chaired the Religious Coalition for Reproductive Choice in 1999. Many Protestant churches have taken pro-choice positions.

that choice each year and decide that abortion is morally correct for them. Hundreds of thousands of women of other faiths make the same decision.[9]

Most pro-choice religious organizations also point out that the United States is not a theocracy (ruled by a god) and that the U.S. Constitution is a secular (nonreligious) document that provides for separation of church and state and the right to privacy. Thus, say pro-choicers, one particular religious point of view should not determine the morality of abortion for everyone.

Pro-Choice Activists

Pro-choice advocates, like their opponents, use the Internet, public protests, legislative initiatives, and various media to get their messages across. Activists are involved in such pro-choice groups as the Alan Guttmacher Institute, the American Association of University Women, the American Civil Liberties Union, the Feminist Majority Foundation, Physicians for Reproductive Choice and Health, the National Abortion Federation, NARAL: Pro-Choice America, the National Organization for Women, Planned Parenthood, and the Religious Coalition for Reproductive Choice.

Also like their opponents, pro-choice advocates support political candidates and government officials who favor their point of view. Many work within political parties. Although the Republican party is often associated with the antiabortion movement, the party includes a Pro-Choice Coalition. Lynn Grefe, national director of the coalition, explained:

> While we work to bring our Party back to a
> position of respect for reproductive health, we join
> the fight to protect the services of Planned
> Parenthood and other providers around the
> country and the world. . . . The goal is clear: it
> should not matter which Party is in control,
> because control must always remain with the
> woman. . . . We dream of the day when there are
> always two pro-choice candidates at the top of
> every ticket. Only then will we have secured the
> rights of all women, regardless of Party politics.[10]

Lawsuits

Often in recent years, pro-choice activists have filed
lawsuits to protect women's right to an abortion. One
such effort by the National Organization for Women
(NOW) was a suit against Joe Scheidler and his mili-
tant group Operation Rescue (now called Operation
Save America). The group—which Scheidler referred
to as the "pro-life mafia"—tried to prevent patients
from entering women's health clinics by attacking
them physically and by forming human blockades—
people arm-in-arm—in front of clinic entrances. In
1998, NOW won a unanimous jury verdict in which
the defendants were found guilty of violating the
Racketeer-Influenced and Corrupt Organizations Act
(RICO) of 1970.

The purpose of the RICO Act is to enable people
who have been hurt financially because of racketeering (gangsterlike activities such as extortion and
forcibly taking property) to seek redress or amends
through the state or federal courts. But the law has

been used to cover diverse crimes. In the NOW case against Scheidler, the court found that antiabortion groups had conspired to shut down abortion clinics through a pattern of racketeering activity. In 1999, an appellate court established a permanent nationwide injunction that bars antiabortion groups from committing violence and intimidation (threats of bodily harm), but protects antiabortion protesters' rights to pray, speak, or hand out leaflets peacefully on public property.

Scheidler appealed the injunction on numerous grounds, including the First Amendment right of free speech. In 2002, the U.S. Supreme Court refused to review Scheidler's appeal, but in 2003 the Court heard the case and ruled in an eight-to-one vote that RICO could not be used to sue Operation Rescue or another group, Pro-Life Action Network. The justices based their decision on their interpretation of extortion. They determined that even though antiabortion groups disrupted and attempted to shut down abortion clinics, their acts did not constitute extortion because they obtained no property.

The Center for Reproductive Law and Policy (CRLP), a nonprofit organization promoting reproductive rights, also helps pro-choice organizations fight legal battles. One CRLP effort involves lawsuits to overturn state bans against D&X procedures. The CRLP was instrumental in an appeal to the U.S. Supreme Court, which in June 2000 upheld a district court's ruling that Nebraska's ban was unconstitutional.

Among other efforts, CRLP opposes treating the "unborn child" as a separate and distinct victim of crime. In addition, on behalf of sixty medical, public health, and other organizations, CRLP petitioned the FDA to make emergency contraception pills available for over-the-counter purchase rather than by prescription only. If ECPs are available to buy without a prescription, half of the three million unintended pregnancies could be prevented, CRLP contends.

Reproductive Freedom Project

Pro-choice activities are also the focus of the Reproductive Freedom Project (RFP) of the American Civil Liberties Union (ACLU). In March 2002, the RFP held a National Day of Appreciation for abortion providers. In her statement, Catherine Weiss, director of the project, declared that

> the threat to providers is not likely to abate in the near future. Given the current political climate, it is particularly important that we increase our vigilance and work to ensure that medical professionals and their patients are safe from violence.
>
> Abortion providers also face continued assaults on the legislative front. In recent years, Congress and many state legislatures have passed laws that threaten doctors with criminal penalties, including prison terms, for providing abortions. . . . Violence, harassment, and legislative interference continue as part of a broad anti-choice effort to eliminate women's access to abortion by, in part, deterring doctors from becoming abortion providers.[11]

Another endeavor of the Reproductive Freedom Project is a major report, *Religious Refusals and Reproductive Rights*. Issued in early 2002, the report details the way religious beliefs in regard to reproductive services are imposed on patients and employees of religiously affiliated clinics and hospitals. For example, a doctor refused to tell a pregnant woman that her prenatal tests showed an abnormal fetus; he withheld the information because he feared the woman would choose to have an abortion. In another instance, a young woman tried to purchase ECPs, but a pharmacist refused to fill the prescription because of his belief that a fertilized egg should not be destroyed.

In these and other cases, according to the report, a health-care provider can adhere to his or her religious beliefs by offering a patient alternative services such as referral to another health-care professional, clinic, or hospital. But, as the report states, "religious or moral convictions" can never "justify endangering a patient's safety." Courts have generally agreed with this position.

For example, a nurse filed a lawsuit against a New Jersey hospital, charging discrimination when she was fired for refusing on religious grounds to assist with induced labor for one pregnant woman and a cesarean section for another. The nurse believed that both procedures put the fetuses' lives at risk even though the pregnant women's lives were in danger. According to the hospital, in one case the nurse's refusal resulted in a serious delay in treating a hemorrhaging (bleeding) patient. The hospital had offered to transfer the nurse to another position in the newborn unit but she did not accept. A federal court ruled that because the hospital

Escorts in Birmingham, Alabama, wait to accompany women into a clinic who might be intimidated by antiabortion protesters. This clinic stayed open despite a bombing at a clinic two blocks away that killed a policeman and injured a nurse.

had tried to accommodate the nurse, there was no religious discrimination.[12]

One section of the report includes the results of public opinion surveys on whether or not caregivers should refuse to treat patients because of religious beliefs:

> Overall, the research shows that Americans . . . believe that denying reproductive health care in the name of religion is wrong: it jeopardizes women's health and lives and goes against the American tradition of religious freedom by forcing religious beliefs on people who do not share them.[13]

Hospital Mergers: A Pro-Choice Concern

A pro-choice concern related to religious refusals is the merger of public hospitals with private hospitals operated by religious groups. These mergers, which were at their peak in the 1990s, include varied arrangements. One hospital might purchase another, for example, or hospitals might work together as partners or affiliates. Why are hospitals combining their services? Primarily because many city-owned and community hospitals across the United States are strapped for funds. They join religiously affiliated hospital networks in order to continue to provide health-care services for local citizens.

Some of the public hospital mergers are with Baptist and Seventh-Day Adventist health-care facilities, which place restrictions on abortion and other reproductive services. But most are with Roman Catholic hospitals that are governed by the Ethical and Religious

Directives for Catholic Health Care Services (ERDs) issued by the National Conference of Catholic Bishops in 1994. The directives not only forbid abortion in a Catholic hospital but also ban providing contraceptive services (including emergency contraception pills for rape victims), performing in vitro fertilization and other fertility treatments, issuing condoms for prevention of AIDS and sexually transmitted diseases, and performing surgical sterilizations to prevent pregnancy. Surgical sterilization includes vasectomy (removing a section of sperm tubes in men) and tubal ligation (cutting and closing off fallopian tubes in women). Thus, a public hospital that previously offered such services would not be permitted to do so after a merger with a religiously affiliated hospital. Catholics for a Free Choice estimated that between 1990 and 2000 there were 159 mergers between Catholic and nonreligious hospitals, and half of these mergers resulted in "a significant reduction in, or outright elimination of, many reproductive health services."[14]

The Religious Coalition for Reproductive Choice (RCRC) condemns the hospital merger trend, calling the situation a "hidden crisis" and noting:

> When a provider with restrictive religious rules dominates most or all health care services in one market, patients are in danger of losing their access to the full range of health services—regardless of their religious affiliation. In a nation founded on religious freedom, it is fundamentally wrong for one religion to impose its beliefs on all citizens.[15]

In some communities where reproductive health services are threatened by mergers, pro-choice groups and other citizens alert the public through forums, petitions, and other means. Sometimes it is not clear to the public that a merger means a hospital will operate under Catholic health-care directives, especially if the hospital has a name that does not sound religious—such as Community Health Partners (Lorain, Ohio), Northridge Hospital Medical Center (Los Angeles, California), or BayCare Consortium (Tampa, Florida).

Public involvement often results in a compromise, some type of accommodation, or ending the merger. A compromise was reached at Brackenridge Hospital in Austin, Texas, for example. The hospital is leased and managed by Catholic Seton Healthcare. Until mid-2001, the hospital provided tubal ligation and other reproductive services, but the U.S. Conference of Catholic Bishops ordered a ban on sterilizations and adherence to its ethical and religious standards at Catholic-affiliated hospitals. As a result, according to the group MergerWatch, the Austin City Council voted in February 2002 to create a separate unit on the fifth floor of the hospital that would be owned and operated by the city. The "hospital within a hospital," which was expected to cost between $8 million and $9.3 million, would provide "reproductive services, including labor and delivery, tubal ligations and contraceptive provision and counseling," MergerWatch reported.[16]

After several years of trying to find a compromise, New Hampshire's Elliot Hospital and Catholic Medical Center agreed to end their merger in early 1999. Although abortions were prohibited at Elliot in

1996, a few were being performed each year, contrary to the Catholic directives. The Catholic Medical Center insisted that Elliot comply with the abortion ban. However, there was an outcry from reproductive health advocates in 1998, after the hospital refused to perform an emergency abortion for a woman who then had to travel eighty miles for the operation.[17]

Mobilizing Pro-Choicers

Ad campaigns are common for both sides in the abortion debate, and in recent years pro-choice groups have developed ads and conducted rallies aimed at mobilizing supporters of reproductive rights. Many pro-choice teenagers and young adults assume that the fight for choice has been won and that abortion will continue to be a legal option for women who choose to end a pregnancy. Yet legal abortions are in jeopardy when legislators pass one law after another to restrict abortion rights or access to women's health clinics.

Serena Cruz, an activist in Boca Raton, Florida, lamented that young women in their twenties are indifferent toward the rights they have earned through the feminist movement and such organizations as NOW and Planned Parenthood. "People of my generation are very consumed with self-interest," Cruz told a reporter. Cruz pointed out that many people in their twenties "don't read the newspaper or watch decent news on TV. They don't know who represents them. They're really materialistic and into consumerism. It's not a conscious thing, but it's out there."[18]

Pro-choicers gather on the steps of the capitol building in Juneau, Alaska, to commemorate the thirtieth anniversary of the Roe v. Wade decision.

To counteract apathy, some pro-choice campaigns have included hard-hitting advertisements in major cities and in college newspapers. For example, the Pro-Choice Public Education Project (PEP) conducted a 2001 campaign designed to dramatize what could happen if abortion becomes illegal. One ad showed a sign over a dirty bathtub identifying it as an "Operating Room." Others depicted a dark alley labeled "Patient Recovery Room" and an abandoned car called an "Abortion Clinic." Flyers for distribution on college campuses are designed to look like official school notices and "equate losing reproductive health

options with the loss of other options as a student."
One flyer, for example, states:

MANDATORY

Effective this semester, all female dorm rooms
must be painted pink. Your resident advisor
will provide you with the necessary supplies.

If a woman loses her reproductive rights, who
knows what rights she could lose next.[19]

Another effort to rally teenagers and young adults
is Spiritual Youth for Reproductive Freedom developed by RCRC and its Spirituality House, an online
campus spirituality center. The center includes a
Study and Action Manual for students who want to
take part in such efforts as keeping women's health
clinics open in the face of intimidating antiabortion
protests.

As pro-choice supporters spread their point of
view, they are frequently countered by pro-lifers, and
vice versa. So the most obvious question is: Will
there ever be any common ground between the two
sides? Some people are working toward that goal.

7

Looking for
Common Ground

A widely respected constitutional scholar, Laurence H. Tribe of Harvard University, titled one of his books *Abortion: The Clash of Absolutes*. Since publication of his book in 1990, the phrase "clash of absolutes" has been used frequently to describe the debate between those who call themselves pro-life and those who say they are pro-choice. To summarize the two conflicting views:

Pro-life

- Human life should be protected from conception.
- Abortion kills an unborn child.

- All human rights are threatened if laws allow unborn children to be killed by abortion.

Pro-choice

- An embryo or fetus is a potential human, but it should not be entitled to "personhood"—or fetal rights.

- A woman should be respected for her ability to make moral and ethical reproductive decisions.

- A woman should not be forced by the state to be a mother.

In some cases, individuals may come together hoping for some kind of dialogue, but this can be a disappointing and frustrating exercise, particularly if advocates on either side expect to change the other's views or positions. However, in spite of seemingly inflexible stands, some groups on both sides have been looking for at least minimum agreement on a few issues.

Preventing Pregnancies

One of the issues on which both sides agree is that reducing unwanted or unexpected pregnancies, particularly among teenagers, can lead to fewer abortions. Although the birth rate for teenagers has declined steadily in recent years, the United States has higher teenage birth and abortion rates than "most Western European countries and some Eastern European countries," according to the Centers for Disease Control and Prevention.[1]

Both public and private groups are dedicated to preventing teen pregnancies. Among them is the nonprofit, nonpartisan National Campaign to Prevent Teen Pregnancy (NCPTP). Founded in 1996, NCPTP has evaluated numerous studies of pregnancy prevention programs to determine which are the most effective. In 2001, NCPTP issued a report, *Emerging Answers: Research Findings On Programs To Reduce Teen Pregnancy.* The report includes an analysis of sex education programs in schools, family planning clinics, and other community efforts, and abstinence-only school courses that teach teenagers to refrain from sex until marriage.

By themselves, the programs brought "mixed results" in terms of pregnancy prevention. But, the report states,

> the research indicates that encouraging abstinence and urging better use of contraception are compatible goals. . . . In fact, effective programs shared two common attributes: (1) being clearly focused on sexual behavior and contraceptive use and (2) delivering a clear message about abstaining from sex as the safest choice for teens and using protection against STDs and pregnancy if a teen is sexually active.[2]

In May 2002, the campaign—along with sponsors *Teen People* magazine and *Teen People Online*—launched the first ever National Day to Prevent Teen Pregnancy. Planned as an annual event, the day is designed to encourage teenagers to think about the importance of postponing pregnancy and parenthood until they are adults and to make a personal

This teenager in Montana is participating in a program that uses "Baby Think It Over." This electronic doll simulates infant behavior—such as crying and sleeping—and records how the student takes care of it. This is one kind of program designed to urge teenagers to put off pregnancy.

commitment to do so. "When it comes to pregnancy, too many teens still think, 'It can't happen to me,'" said Sarah Brown, the National Campaign's director. "The truth is that 'it' happens to nearly one million young women each year."[3]

More than eighty prominent national organizations, from the AMA to the YWCA, were National Day partners, helping to publicize an online quiz that presents realistic situations, such as peer pressure to have sex and out-of-control parties, and asks teens to choose the best behavior to prevent pregnancies. Why was the activity placed online? Because 17 million teenagers aged twelve to seventeen use the Internet, and many of them look there for health information. "The online nature of the National Day quiz also allows for widespread dissemination because teens can pass it onto their friends through emails and instant messaging," the sponsors noted.[4]

Public Conversations Project

While efforts to prevent teen pregnancies and abortions continue, other groups attempt to create dialogue between opposing groups. For example, the Public Conversations Project (PCP), which is based in Boston, initiates dialogues about divisive public issues. PCP was instrumental in bringing together pro-choice and pro-life advocates following a rampage in December 1994 by gunman John Salvi, who killed two abortion clinic workers and wounded five in the Boston, Massachusetts, area. After the shootings, there were numerous calls for talks between leaders of pro-choice and pro-life groups in Massachusetts. Six women—an Episcopal minister, the director of the Center for Reproductive Law and Policy, the president of Women Affirming Life, the director of the Massachusetts National Abortion and Reproductive Rights Action League, the past president of the Massachusetts Citizens for Life, and the director of the Pro-Life Office of the Catholic Archdiocese in

Boston—met for the first time in September 1995. These three pro-life and three pro-choice leaders conducted a private conversation, and other dialogues followed over a period that spanned five and a half years. Their meetings were held in secret because the women were getting together as individuals rather than representatives of their various organizations and because they were afraid that people might try to stop the meetings with violence.

What did the women hope to accomplish? In a 2001 feature for the *Boston Globe,* the women explained that they wanted

> to communicate openly with our opponents, away from the polarizing spotlight of media coverage; to build relationships of mutual respect and understanding; to help deescalate the rhetoric of the abortion controversy; and, of course, to reduce the risk of future shootings.[5]

Even as they spelled out their high-minded goals, the women also expressed anxiety and fear about meeting with the "enemy." PCP facilitators moderated all the meetings and enforced strict ground rules, one of which was to agree not to argue for a particular cause. Another rule was to use terms acceptable to all. For example, the pro-choice women opposed using the term "unborn baby," while the pro-life women were against the term "fetus." The compromise that evolved was "human fetus."

When the women's report was published in the *Boston Globe,* it was the first public disclosure of their meetings. All the women contributed to the feature and collectively concluded, "These conversations revealed a deep divide. We saw that our differences on abortion reflect two world views that are irreconcilable." However, they noted that their meetings allowed them to see their opponents' "dignity and goodness" and to engage in "candid conversations" that made their "thinking sharper and . . . language more precise."[6] In the end, they gained respect and trust for each other while at the same time reaffirming their own views on abortion.

The public response to the article was overwhelmingly positive, with praise for the rational way in which the women discussed their differences. Many of the e-mails that the newspaper received are posted along with the feature article on the PCP's Web site.[7]

Unanswered Questions

In spite of efforts to find common ground in the abortion debate, questions continue to crop up about such issues as:

- Will abortions be increasingly restricted in the United States?

- Who should determine what kind of reproductive health care a woman will receive?

- How can the language used to talk about reproductive issues be clarified and become less emotional?

- What should be done with frozen embryos that parents no longer want or need?

- How will advances in medical technology and increasing knowledge about the fetus affect abortion decisions?

- What can be done to assure that every child born is wanted?

- How can violence associated with abortion debates be reduced?

- How can people on both sides of the abortion debate respectfully disagree?

- When will long-term national studies be conducted to determine the physical and psychological aftereffects of abortion?

No one can predict exactly what answers will be given to such questions, but there is little doubt that they will be discussed now and in the future. Rational discussion on the subject can lead to a better understanding of responsible decision-making, which in itself requires weighing options. In an open, democratic society, those options vary in regard to ending a pregnancy, becoming a parent, or considering other reproductive issues. Perhaps thoughtful discussion will at least move the abortion debate beyond bitter accusations to respect for diverse opinions.

Chapter Notes

Chapter 1. Struggling With Abortion Dilemmas

1. Rachel K. Jones, Jacqueline E. Darroch and Stanley K. Henshaw, "Patterns in the Socioeconomic Characteristics of Women Obtaining Abortions in 2000–2001," *Perspectives on Sexual and Reproductive Health*, September–October 2002, p. 226.

2. U.S. Department of Health and Human Services, "Interim Report Says Abstinence Programs Are 'Changing The Local Landscape' in Teen Pregnancy Prevention Efforts," news release, April 23, 2002, <http://www.hhs.gov/news/press/2002pres/20020423.html> (February 17, 2003).

3. Kate Zernike, "30 Years After Roe v. Wade, New Trends but the Old Debate," *The New York Times*, January 20, 2003, p. A1.

4. Angela Bonavoglia, ed., *The Choices We Made: Twenty-Five Women and Men Speak Out About Abortion* (New York: Random House, 1991), pp. 182–183.

5. Annette Tomal, "The Effect of Religious Membership on Teen Abortion Rates," *Journal of Youth and Adolescence*, February 2001, p. 103.

Chapter 2. History of Abortion and Abortion Laws

1. Suzanne Wymelenberg for the Institute of Medicine, *Science and Babies: Private Decisions, Public Dilemmas* (Washington, D.C.: National Academy Press, 1990), pp. 41–42.

2. "Abortion in Law, History, and Religion," booklet (Toronto, Canada: Childbirth by Choice Trust, 1995), p. 6.

3. K. Kaufmann, *The Abortion Resource Handbook* (New York: Simon & Schuster/Fireside, 1997), p. 134.

4. Associated Press, "Toxic Pennyroyal Sometimes Used As Abortifacient," *Seattle Post-Intelligencer,* October 27, 1996, <http://www.w-cpc.org/news/seattle10-96.html> (February 24, 2003).

5. Timothy Crumrin, "Her Daily Concern: Women's Health Issues in Early 19th-Century Indiana," n.d., <http://www.connerprairie.org/historyonline/whlh.html> (June 10, 2003).

6. Leslie J. Reagan, *When Abortion Was A Crime: Women, Medicine, and the Law in the United States, 1867–1973* (Berkeley: University of California Press, 1997), p.11; see also American Civil Liberties Union, "The Right to Choose at 25: Looking Back and Ahead," January 31, 1998, <http://www.aclu.org/Reproductive Rights/ReproductiveRights.cfm?ID=9006&c=30> (June 10, 2003).

7. American Civil Liberties Union.

8. California Abortion Rights Action League, "1821–1955: The Silent Decades," n.d., <http://www.choice.org/roevwade/TLpg2.html> (June 10, 2003).

9. Ibid.; see also Fredrick N. Dyer, "Pro-Life Physician Horatio Robinson Storer: Your Ancestors, and You," n.d., <http://www.abortionessay.com/files/yourancestors.html> (June 10, 2003).

10. Reagan, p. 36.

11. Emma Goldman, *Living My Life* (New York: New American Library, 1977), p.185.

12. Reagan, pp. 36, 41.

13. David J. Garrow, "Abortion Before and After Roe v. Wade: An Historical Perspective," *Albany Law Review,* Spring 1999, p. 183.

14. American Civil Liberties Union.

15. Childbirth by Choice, eds., *No Choice: Canadian Women Tell Their Stories of Illegal Abortion* (Toronto, Canada: Childbirth by Choice Trust, 1998), p. 13.

16. Ibid., p. 47.

••

17. Ibid., p. 50.

18. Angela Bonavoglia, ed., *The Choices We Made: Twenty-Five Women and Men Speak Out About Abortion* (New York: Random House, 1991), pp. 116–117.

19. Reagan, pp. 221–222.

20. American Civil Liberties Union.

21. Centers for Disease Control and Prevention, *CDC Surveillance Summaries,* July 30, 1999, p. 1.

22. Centers for Disease Control and Prevention, "Fact Sheet: Pregnancy-Related Deaths in the United States, 1987–1990," 1997, <http://www.cdc.gov/nccdphp/drh/mh_prvleath.htm> (June 10, 2003).

23. The Alan Guttmacher Institute, "Facts in Brief: Induced Abortion," February 2000, <http://www.agiusa.org/pubs/fb_induced_abortion.html> (June 9, 2003).

24. *Roe et al* v. *Wade,* District Attorney of Dallas County, Appeal from the United States District Court for the Northern District of Texas, No. 70-18, Argued December 13, 1971, Reargued October 11, 1972, Decided January 22, 1973.

25. U.S. Supreme Court, *Doe* v. *Bolton,* 410 U.S. 179 (1973), Argued December 13, 1971, Reargued October 11, 1972, Decided January 22, 1973.

26. The Alan Guttmacher Institute, "Issues in Brief: Challenges Facing Family Planning Clinics and Title X," 2001, <http://www.agi-usa.org/pubs/ib_3-01.html> (June 10, 2003).

Chapter 3. Abortion Today

1. Joy Herndon, Lilo T. Strauss, Sara Whitchead, Wilda Y. Parker, Linda Bartlett, and Suzanne Zane, "Abortion Surveillance—United States 1998," Division of Reproductive Health, National Center for Chronic Disease Prevention and Health Promotion, June 7, 2002, <http://www.cdc.gov/mmwr/preview/mmwrhtml/ss5103a1.htm> (June 10, 2003).

2. The Alan Guttmacher Institute, "Facts in Brief—Induced Abortion," 2002, <http://www.agi-usa.org/pubs/fb_induced_abortion.pdf> (June 10, 2003); see also Bernadine Healy, *A New Prescription for Women's Health: Getting the Best Medical Care in a Man's World* (New York: Viking, 1995), p. 114.

3. Bernadine Healy.

4. *The Planned Parenthood Women's Health Encyclopedia* (New York: Crown, 1996), p. 336.

5. The Alan Guttmacher Institute.

6. Jon Knowles (revised by Danielle Dimitrov), "Medical Abortion—Questions and Answers," June 2002, <http://www.plannedparenthood.org/ABORTION/medicalabortion.html> (June 9, 2003).

7. Richard U. Hausknecht, "Methotrexate and Misoprostol to Terminate Early Pregnancy," *New England Journal of Medicine,* August 31, 1995, Abstract, p. 537.

8. Ellen Chesler, "The Abortion Debate: Finding Common Ground," *Ideas for an Open Society* (newsletter of the Open Society Institute), May–June 2001, <http://www.soros.org/ideas/summer01/ideas_finding.html> (June 10, 2003).

9. ReligiousTolerance.org, "Non-surgical, Medically Induced Abortions: The RU-486 Abortion Pill," <http://www.religioustolerance.org/aboru486.htm> (June 10, 2003).

10. Rachel K. Jones and Stanley K. Henshaw, "Mifepristone for Early Medical Abortion: Experiences in France, Great Britain and Sweden," *Perspectives on Sexual and Reproductive Health,* May–June 2002, p. 154.

11. BSS International, "Non-Surgical Medical Abortion," n.d., <http://www.drbenjamin.com/2.html> (June 9, 2003); see also Danco Laboratories, "Dear Healthcare Professional Letter," September 28, 2000, <http://www.fda.gov/medwatch/SAFETY/2002/mifeprex_deardoc.pdf> (June 9, 2003).

12. Stephen L. Fielding, Emme Edmunds and Eric A. Schaff, "Having an Abortion Using Mifepristone and Home Misoprostol: A Qualitative Analysis of Women's Experiences," *Family Planning Perspectives,* January–February 2002, p. 34.

13. The Alan Guttmacher Institute.

14. Planned Parenthood Federation of America, "How Abortion is Provided," 2002, <http://www.planned parenthood.org/library/ABORTION/howabort_fact.html> (June 10, 2003).

15. Janet E. Gans Epner, Harry S. Jonas, and Daniel L. Seckinger, "Late-term Abortion," *Journal of the American Medical Association,* August 26, 1998, pp. 724–729.

16. University of North Carolina Chapel Hill News Service, "Doctors Say Abortion 'Informed Consent' Should Include Details On Physical, Psychological Effects," press release, January 24, 2003, <http://www.unc.edu/news/ newsserv/research/jan03/thorp012403.html> (June 9, 2003); see also John M. Thorp, Jr., Katherine E. Hartmann, and Elizabeth Shadigian, "Long-Term Physical and Psychological Health Consequences of Induced Abortion: Review of the Evidence," *Obstetrical & Gynecological Survey,* January 2003, pp. 67–79.

Chapter 4. The Abortion Debate

1. ReligiousTolerance.org, "Abortion: Public Opinion Polls: Year 2003," 2003, <http://www.religioustolerance. org/abo_poll5.htm> (June 9, 2003).

2. Health on the Net Foundation, "Most Americans Support Abortion, Polls Say," January 22, 2003, <http:// www.hon.ch/News/HSN/511397.html> (June 10, 2003).

3. ReligiousTolerance.org, "Jewish Beliefs About Abortion," 2002, <http://www.religioustolerance.org/ jud_abor.htm> (June 10, 2003).

4. Carl Sagan, *Billions and Billions: Thoughts on Life and Death at the Brink of the Millennium* (New York: Random House, 1997), p. 176.

5. Neuroscience for Kids, "Types of Neurons (Nerve Cells)," 2003, <http://faculty.washington.edu/chudler/cells.html> (February 23, 2003); see also Think and Grow, "Dendrites—Flowers of Intelligence," n.d., <http://tagtoys.com/html/dendrites.htm> (June 10, 2003).

6. Religious Coalition for Reproductive Choice, "Speak Out Against the Deceptive 'Unborn Victims of Violence Act,'" 2002, <http://www.rcrc.org/actioncenter/UVVA.htm> (June 10, 2003).

7. American Civil Liberties Union, "Coercive and Punitive Governmental Responses to Women's Conduct During Pregnancy," September 30, 1997, <http://www.aclu.org/ReproductiveRights/ReproductiveRights.cfm?ID=9054&c=144> (June 10, 2003).

8. Ibid.

9. Cynthia Dailard and Elizabeth Nash, "State Responses to Substance Abuse Among Pregnant Women," The Alan Guttmacher Institute, December 2000, <http://www.agi-usa.org/pubs/ib_006.html> (June 10, 2003).

10. ACLU Feature, "Policing Pregnancy: Ferguson v. City of Charleston," October 3, 2000, <http://archive.aclu.org/features/f100300a.html> (June 10, 2003).

11. American Civil Liberties Union, "In Victory for Privacy, Supreme Court Rejects State's Drug Testing of Pregnant Women," press release, March 21, 2001, <http://archive.aclu.org/news/2001/n032101a.html> (June 10, 2003).

12. American Civil Liberties Union, "American Civil Liberties Union: ACLU Denounces House Passage of Safe Abortion Procedures Ban; Says Lawsuit Planned to Protect Women and Doctors," press release, June 5, 2003, <http://www.aclu.org/ReproductiveRights/ReproductiveRights.cfm?ID=12816&c=148> (August 20, 2003).

13. The Alan Guttmacher Institute, "State Policies in Brief: Parental Involvement in Minors' Abortions,"

January 1, 2002, <http://www.agi-usa.org/pubs/spib_ARR.pdf> (June 10, 2003).

14. K. Kaufmann, *The Abortion Resource Handbook* (New York: Fireside/Simon & Schuster, 1997), p. 45.

15. David Oliver Relin, "Old Enough to Choose?" *Scholastic Update,* April 10, 1990, p. 13.

16. National Abortion Rights Action League, "Walk in Her Shoes: Becky," n.d., <http://www.naral.org/generation/walk/wis_1_true.html> (June 11, 2003).

17. Feminists for Life of America, "Reflections on the Becky Bell Tragedy," 2000, <http://www.feministsforlife.org/FFL_topics/after/beckbell.htm> (June 10, 2003).

18. American Association of University Women, "Minors' Access to Reproductive Services," January 2002, <http://www.aauw.org/takeaction/policyissues/minors_access.cfm> (June 9, 2003).

19. American Medical Association, Code of Medical Ethics, "Mandatory Parental Consent to Abortion," adopted June 1992, <http://imc.gsm.com/demos/dddemo/consult/parental.htm> (June 10, 2003).

20. "Mandatory Parental Consent to Abortion," *The Journal of the American Medical Association,* January 6, 1993, pp. 82–86.

Chapter 5. The Pro-Life View

1. B.A. Robinson, ReligiousTolerance.org, "Definitions of Terms About Pregnancy and Abortion," n.d., <http://www.religioustolerance.org/abo_defn.htm> (June 10, 2003).

2. "Common Questions People Ask about Islam," n.d., <http://www.angelfire.com/indie/csesanker/ISLAM%20AND%20ABORTION.htm> (June 10, 2003).

3. Nat Hentoff, "Pro Choice Bigots," *The New Republic,* November 30, 1992, <http://prolife.liberals.com/articles/hentoff.html> (June 10, 2003).

4. "Natural Rights," n.d., <http://www.geocities.com/sonyaelflady/nrmission.htm> (June 10, 2003).

5. Americans United for Life, "30 Years of Abortion and Its Impact on Women," n.d., <http://www.unitedforlife.org> (June 9, 2003).

6. LifeAthletes.org, "Who We Are," n.d., <http://www.lifeathletes.org/0008/who_we_are.asp> (June 10, 2003).

7. Pro-Life Alliance of Gays and Lesbians, "Human Rights Starts When Human Life Begins" (brochure), n.d., <http://www.plagal.org/brochures/white.pdf> (June 9, 2003).

8. Lydia Saad, "Public Opinion About Abortion—An In-Depth Review," Gallup Poll Special Report, January 22, 2002, <http://www.gallup.com/poll/specialReports/poll Summaries/sr020122.asp> (June 10, 2003).

9. Derrick Jones, "Reflections of a College Kid (Becoming a Pro-life Activist)," *National Right to Life News,* January 2002, <http://www.nrlc.org/news/2002/NRL01/derrik.html> (February 23, 2003).

10. Ed Rivet, "Roe v. Wade Remembrance—29 Years," speech at Michigan pro-life rally, January 20, 2002, <http://www.faithmag.com/todaysfaith/2002/1-26-02.html> (June 10, 2003).

11. Pro-life Berks, January 2002 Newsletter, <http://www.prolifeberks.org/jan02newsletter.htm> (June 10, 2003).

12. National Abortion Federation, "Analysis of Trends of Violence and Disruption Against Reproductive Health Care Clinics for 2002," February 6, 2003, <http://www.prochoice.org> (February 23, 2003).

13. Anne Bower, "Soldier in the Army of God," *Albion Monitor,* February 18, 1996, <http://www.monitor.net/monitor/abortion/abortionsoldier.html> (June 10, 2003).

14. Dan Horn, "Waagner Claims Divine Direction," *The Cincinnati Enquirer,* April 18, 2002, <http://www.enquirer.com/editions/2002/04/18/loc_waagner_claims.html> (June 10, 2003).

15. Neal Horsley, "Visualize Abortionists on Trial: The

Nuremberg Files," n.d., <http://www.christiangallery.com/atrocity/> (June 10, 2003).

16. Frederick Clarkson, "A Radical Antiabortionist Backs Down," *Salon.com,* June 21, 2002, <http://www.salon.com/news/feature/2002/06/21/abortion/index_np.html> (June 10, 2003).

17. American Life League, "In Vitro Fertilization," n.d., <http://www.all.org/issues/ivf.htm> (June 10, 2003).

18. "Embryonic Stem Cells: Research at UW-Madison," 2001, <http://www.news.wisc.edu/packages/stemcells/index.html?get-facts#1> (June 10, 2003).

19. George W. Bush, "Remarks by the President on Stem Cell Research," press release, August 9, 2001, <http://www.whitehouse.gov/news/releases/2001/08/2001080 9-2.html> (June 10, 2003).

20. Ted Halstead and Michael Lind, "Double Jeopardy: Can It Be a Crime to Seek Treatment For A Deadly Disease? Congress Seems to Think So," *Washington Post,* May 5, 2002, p. B4.

21. National Institutes of Health, "Stem Cells: A Primer," September 2002, <http://www.nih.gov/news/stemcell/primer.htm> (June 10, 2003).

22. Concerned Women for America, press release, February 2, 2003, <http://www.cwfa.org/articledisplay.asp?id=3277&department=MEDIA&categoryid=life> (June 10, 2003).

Chapter 6. The Pro-Choice View

1. Joyce Arthur, "No, Virginia, Abortion is NOT Genocide," *The Humanist,* July 2000, p. 20.

2. "PEP and the Media," Pro-Choice Public Education Project, n.d., <http://www.protectchoice. org/> (June 10, 2003).

3. Kate Michelman, Remarks at NARAL's *Roe* v. *Wade* 30th Anniversary Celebration, January 21, 2003, <http://www.naral.org/about/newsroom/pressrelease/20030122_roespeech.cfm> (June 10, 2003).

4. "How Can You Be Pro-Choice and Republican?" Republican Pro-Choice Coalition, n.d., <http://www.rpcc.org/faq9.html> (June 10, 2003).

5. Steve Neal, "Pro-Choice Champion Michelman in Battle for the Long Haul," *Chicago Sun-Times,* April 30, 2003.

6. Public Broadcasting System, "NOW with Bill Moyers," May 13, 2003, <http://www.pbs.org/now/transcript/transcript220_full.html> (June 10, 2003).

7. Religious Coalition for Reproductive Choice, Fact Sheet, n.d., <http://www.rcrc.org/rcrc/fact sheet.html> (June 10, 2003).

8. Dr. Paul D. Simons, "Personhood, the Bible, and the Abortion Debate," n.d., <http://www.rcrc.org/religion/es3/comp.html> (June 10, 2003).

9. Frances Kissling, "Is There a Choice?" *Newsday* (Letters to the Editor), May 2, 2001, <http://www.cath4choice.org/new/opeds/050201IsThereAChoice.htm> (June 10, 2003).

10. Lynn Grefe, "GOP Pro-Choicers Would Rather Fight than Switch," Spring 2001, <http://www.wcla.org/01-spring/gop.html> (June 10, 2003).

11. Catherine Weiss, "ACLU Salutes Abortion Providers On National Day of Appreciation," press release, March 10, 2002.

12. Catherine Weiss, Caitlin Borgmann, Lorraine Kenny, Julie Sternberg, and Margaret Crosby, *Religious Refusals and Reproductive Rights: ACLU Reproductive Freedom Project* (New York: American Civil Liberties Union, 2002), p. 10.

13. Ibid., p. 23.

14. Catholics for a Free Choice, "Catholic Health Care—Hospital Mergers in the USA," n.d., <http://www.cath4choice.org/nobandwidth/English/healthmergers.htm> (June 10, 2003).

15. Religious Coalition for Reproductive Choice, "Hospital Mergers: The Hidden Crisis," n.d., <http://

www.rcrc.org/pubs/speakout/merge.html> (June 10, 2003).

16. "Current Threats: Brackenridge Hospital," MergerWatch, n.d., <http://www.mergerwatch.org/hospitals/Austin.html> (June 10, 2003).

17. Catholics for a Free Choice.

18. Victor Greto, "NOW Aims to Revitalize Energize Movement in S. Florida," Knight-Ridder/Tribune News Service, April 5, 2002.

19. Pro-Choice Public Education Project, "Campus Handouts," 2001, <http://www.protectchoice.org/ads/posters/PEP_ad2.pdf> (June 10, 2003).

Chapter 7. Looking for Common Ground

1. Centers for Disease Control and Prevention, *Morbidity and Mortality Weekly Report,* July 30, 1999, p. 7.

2. Douglas Kirby, *Emerging Answers: Research Findings on Programs to Reduce Teen Pregnancy* (Washington, D.C.: National Campaign to Prevent Teen Pregnancy, May 2001), p. 18.

3. National Campaign to Prevent Teen Pregnancy, "Teens Nationwide To Participate in the First-Ever National Day to Prevent Teen Pregnancy," press release, May 7, 2002, <http://www.teenpregnancy.org/about/announcements/pr/2002/natday.asp> (June 10, 2003).

4. Ibid.

5. Anne Fowler, Nicki Nichols Gamble, Frances X. Hogan, Melissa Kogut, Madeline McComish, and Barbara Thorp, "Talking with the Enemy," *The Boston Globe,* January 28, 2001, p. F1, <http://www.public conversations.org/pcp/resources/resource_detail.asp?ref_id=102> (June 10, 2003).

6. Ibid.

7. "Boston Prochoice and Prolife Leaders' Dialogue: Public Response," Public Conversations Project, 2001, <http://www.publicconversations.org/pcp/index.asp?page_id=169&catid=50> (June 10, 2003).

Glossary

abortifacient—A drug or herb that can cause an abortion.

amniocentesis—A test to determine whether the fetus has any abnormalities.

cervix—The neck or outer end of the uterus.

cesarean section (C-section)—A surgical procedure to deliver a baby.

chromosome—Genetic material in a cell.

contraceptive—Any drug, device, or technique used to prevent conception or pregnancy.

crisis pregnancy center—A center that is usually staffed with counselors who offer alternatives to abortion and practical help for pregnant women.

curettage—The process of using a tool called a curette to remove tissue from the wall of the uterus.

dilation and evacuation (D&E)—An abortion process in which the cervix is dilated and a fetus and placenta tissue are removed by suction curettage.

ectopic pregnancy—An abnormal and dangerous condition in which a pregnancy develops in a fallopian tube or in the abdominal cavity instead of inside the uterus.

elective abortion—An abortion performed at the wish or choice of the woman.

embryo—The earliest stage of pregnancy from two weeks after conception to the eighth week.

emergency contraception pills (ECPs)—Birth control pills taken within seventy-two hours after unprotected sexual intercourse.

fertilization—The process that begins when a male sperm and female egg make contact; conception.

fetus—The developing human in the womb from nine weeks after conception to birth.

implantation—The attachment of the fertilized egg to the wall of the uterus.

intact dilation and extraction (D&X)—A rare late-term abortion process in which the brain and spinal fluid from the fetus are removed before extracting it.

in vitro fertilization—An artificial means of conception in which the egg and sperm are combined in a laboratory petri dish.

nonsectarian—Not affiliated with a particular religious group.

sterilization—Surgery to make a woman or man sterile (unable to reproduce).

trimester—A period of three months.

tubal ligation—An operation to tie or cut a woman's fallopian tubes to cause sterilization.

vasectomy—A surgical process to remove a section of the male sperm tube to cause sterilization.

viability—The ability of the developing fetus to live on its own outside the womb, usually between 21 and 28 weeks after conception.

zygote—A single-celled organism formed after an egg is fertilized.

For More Information

The Alan Guttmacher
Institute
120 Wall Street
21st Floor
New York, N.Y. 10005
(212) 248-1111

1120 Connecticut
Avenue, NW
Suite 460
Washington, D.C.
20036
(202) 296-4012

American Life League
P.O. Box 1350
Stafford, Va. 22555
(540) 659-4171

Americans United for Life
310 S. Peoria Street
Suite 300
Chicago, Ill.
60607-3534
(312) 492-7234

Catholics for a Free Choice
1436 U Street, NW
Suite 301
Washington, D.C.
20009-3997
(202) 986-6093

Feminists for Life of America
733 15th Street, NW
Suite 1100
Washington, D.C.
20005
(202) 737-3352

NARAL Pro-Choice America
1156 15th Street
Suite 700
Washington, D.C.
20005
(202) 973-3000

National Right to Life
Committee
512 10th St., NW
Washington, D.C.
20004
(202) 626-8800

Planned Parenthood
Federation of America
810 Seventh Avenue
New York, N.Y. 10019
(212) 541-7800

U.S. Centers for Disease
Control and Prevention
1600 Clifton Road
Atlanta, Ga. 30333
(404) 639-3311

Further Reading

Books

Buckingham, Robert and Mary P. Derby. *I'm Pregnant, Now What Do I Do?* Amherst, Mass.: Prometheus Books, 1997.

Knapp, Lynette, ed. *The Abortion Controversy.* Farmington Hills, Mich.: Greenhaven, 2001.

Lassieur, Allison. *Abortion.* Farmington Hills, Mich.: Gale Group, 2001.

Peacock, Judith. *Abstinence: Postponing Sexual Involvement.* Mankato, Minn.: Capstone Press, 2000.

Romaine, Deborah S. *Roe v. Wade: Abortion and the Supreme Court.* Farmington Hills, Mich.: Gale Group, 1998.

Internet Addresses

The Alan Guttmacher Institute
<http://www.agi-usa.org>

National Day to Prevent Teen Pregnancy
<http://www.teenpregnancy.org/national/pdf/2005/2005Brochure.pdf>

National Right to Life Committee
<http://www.nrlc.org>

Index